THE BATTLE FOR THE SEED

Spiritual Strategy
To Preserve Our Children

Dr. Patricia Morgan

Destiny Image Publishers
P.O. Box 310
Shippensburg, PA 17257

"Speaking to the Purposes of God for this Generation"

ISBN 1-56043-099-0

For Worldwide Distribution
Printed in the U.S.A.

Second Printing:1992

TABLE OF CONTENTS

Dedication

To our foster children, for whom I battle and who continue to display the Father's victory and joy.

To our children — Cathy, Colin, Carrington and Christopher — whose growth in ability to fight their own battles encourages and allows us to strategize for our nation's children.

Acknowledgements

To the Holy Spirit, my Friend, Encourager and Guide, Who commissioned this work and Who continues to be my source of power for the BATTLE.

To my husband, Peter, who lovingly facilitated this ministry, for his companionship and careful attention to my personal battle for our seed.

To Oral and Richard Roberts, Gary North, Myles Munroe, Carlton Pearson, Carolyn Harrell, Sarah Jordan-Powell, Pam Vinnett and Larry Walker, whose dedication to their own ministries has been a source of inspiration and learning.

To our Third World Covenant brethren with whose partnership we determine to restore our nations and our generation.

Foreword

The condition of human society should be of tremendous concern to all of us — no matter what our station in life. The "hope factor" in our communities has been absorbed by the deteriorating social, economic, political, spiritual and moral state of our nations.

Uncertainty, insecurity, disillusionment, confusion, frustration and fear have gripped entire societies, causing many to ask: "Is there a future? What will it be like? How can we secure it?"

This book addresses these very serious questions and the vital issue of preserving our children, our SEED, in the middle of this turbulent generation. Pat Morgan offers sound advice that all of us must heed. The principles presented are time-tested and will work for our generation as we take our position in the . . . BATTLE FOR THE SEED.

The richest resource of every nation is the next generation incubating in its national womb — the children, the youth, the babies. Every nation is pregnant with a future generation, and the neglect of that generation is abuse of the future. If the future is to be changed, the children are the agency through whom change will come.

The power to change the future is with us in the present. God always goes after the seed within the fruit. In every seed, there is not just a tree but a forest. Have you noticed that whenever God wanted to fulfill His purpose He would give birth to a child? . . . Moses, Jacob, John the Baptist, Jesus. And have you noticed that whenever Satan attempts to thwart God's purpose, he goes after the children . . . the next generation?

We must therefore, at all cost, understand, protect and preserve the "SEED" — the next generation. Children are not only the heritage of the Lord but they are also the future of the present. We can determine what kind of future our nations will have by what we transmit to them.

Every nation is pregnant with a generation, and we all know that *the condition of the mother affects the health of the baby*. Whatever the mother eats, drinks, or inhales will be transferred to the offspring. In essence, the diet of the nation will manifest in the next generation. We must therefore not be guilty of generational abortion or be the cause of national miscarriage.

I recommend this book to all who desire to fulfill their responsibility to the next generation and to fulfill God's purpose in this planet.

Dr. Myles Munroe
Nassau, Bahamas

Introduction

Look in your daily newspaper. Listen to the television newscast. Our youth and children are dying. Is this some grand diabolical plot to thwart God's plan for the deliverance of families and nations?

I have discovered that God and this arch-enemy are in a head-on BATTLE FOR THE SEED, our children. The extent to which Satan prevails is in direct proportion to our knowledge and use of **supernatural strategies** to preserve our children!

After years of professional study, pastoral ministry with my husband, and two decades of child-rearing, I have something that must be said. The Spirit of the Lord won't let me wait any longer!

Man of God, woman of God, you are a vital part of God's marvelous plan to save the nations. Your efforts (or lack of them) within your own family unit directly affect its role within your nation.

It is the purpose of God to bring forth righteousness on His created earth. He will do this by the raising up of our righteous seed. It is therefore our responsibility as parents to collaborate with God in this mission.

This book speaks directly to Christian men and women of every nation, but I pray that it will be read by everyone called to help preserve our seed — our children — God's Nation Builders.

1
Raise A Child, Shape A Nation

For I the Lord love judgment, I hate robbery for burnt offering; and I will direct their work in truth, and I will make an everlasting covenant with them.

And their seed shall be known among the Gentiles, and their offspring among the people: all that see them shall acknowledge them, that they are the seed which the Lord hath blessed.

Isaiah 61:8,9

Our lives are intricately bound up with the life of our nation. Every day we face conditions and circumstances that we must overcome in order to preserve the life of our sons and daughters, and indeed, of our nation.

Consider the shock faced by thousands of mothers across the globe when war forced its way into their lives during the Persian Gulf crisis. They watched their children walk out the door, and then endured endless months of heartache and fear, wondering if they would ever see their faces again. Prayer suddenly became fashionable, women pleading for their threatened seed.

When I look about me and see decay in my nation, in our families and in our cities, I feel a supernatural stirring in my heart. In every nation on the earth, we see corruption, bribery, idolatry, the occult, poverty and spiritual ignorance, blatant sin (even in the lives of believers) and unrepentance rise unrestrained. These nations stand in judgment before a righteous God.

As a mother of four teenagers, a homemaker within a nation, and a woman committed to the building up of

God's kingdom on this earth, I refuse to be deaf, dumb and blind!

We have a national problem. God has not changed. In the history of the Israelites, and as a result of national unrighteousness and injustice, God's wrath was released upon His own people. I believe His hand is heavy in this hour on the Caribbean Islands, as well as upon other nations of the world. When we see the destruction wrought by natural disasters such as earthquakes and hurricanes and the decadence of our cities, we must ask the question, "Has the hand of God's protection and mercy lifted from us because He can no longer look upon the corruption of cities and nations?"

As parents bringing up children in our nations, we can no longer distance ourselves from the things which are occurring right before our very eyes. As a result of not only seeing but painfully experiencing some of these calamities, I have sought the face of God. It is through His Word, dreams and visions that He has impressed upon my spirit the great urgency we face if our children are to survive.

It is my prayer that God's Spirit will quicken you so that you will not distance yourself from your people - your own flesh and blood, yes, but also from the children of your nation. The question is: "What are we to do about the situations we face, such as the impending judgment of a holy God on an unrighteous generation?"

One such threat is godless, humanistic ideologies. Not long ago, God gave me a vision. I was thrown to the ground, helpless and powerless. On the top of the highest hills the spokesmen stood and bellowed out, loudly and clearly, their heretical proclamations. I looked down and saw my husband and other leaders of the Body of Christ silenced and cast down to the valleys below. I saw women ravished and everywhere children were perishing.

4

This vision is still alive in my heart and propels me to action as a woman of God in my nation and on behalf of my men and children. I know that I cannot remain silent because this vision is like fire in my bones. The nations are dying. Our sons and daughters are being engulfed by the voices of the teachers of godless ideologies. There is hopelessness, and there is despair. What can we do about it?

In 1977, God gave a prophetic word in the nation of Trinidad and Tobago. It was spoken to the men and women of the Caribbean nations by Babsie Bleasdale.

" 'The living waters of My Spirit,' saith the Lord, 'flood this land to mingle with the waters of the Caribbean. Oh, My people, how I long to draw you to Myself. I brought you from many nations to create of you one people. You are My covenant people of the Twentieth Century. My heart delights to see men and women of the Caribbean pass by, of many hues, colors, persuasions — all one in Me.

" 'I long to heal your nostrils from the smell of the slave ships. I long to heal your ears from the crack of the slave driver's whip. I long to heal you in the deep recesses of your heart. I long to make you whole,' saith the Lord, 'to make you My people, a people of whom I can be very proud that you may know Me.

" 'I am God, and I shall bring men and women from nations across the seas to see men of the Caribbean pass by, My people. And they shall know that I am God and I alone could do this thing...weave many races into one people and make men of all colors a people, a holy people, My people.' "

It is possible for a people to inherit, from events in the history of their nation, a kind of national malaise, the seeds of which were planted hundreds of years before, and whose roots become more deeply embedded in the soils of oppression.

Then God spoke again:

> "I could not say to many of you, 'Let your elders be pure and holy,' for your elders have all been tainted. But I long to heal you from the shame of your bastardy. I want to wash your faces clean, and I want to make you holy. 'Out of the Magdalenes and the Zacchaeuses, I shall raise up My people,' saith the Lord, 'and all will know that I am God and that I dwell with My people.' "

This prophetic word reflects, with deep pathos, the heart of a Father God who longs to heal men and women of every nation from personal and cultural hurts and from recurring generational pain. God waits to erase those emotional scars, whether national or personal, inflicted by slavery or by an individual Magdalene/Zacchaeus experience.

God has said that He is about to raise up and "show off" His Magdalenes and His Zacchaeuses. But first, our lives must be wrapped up in Him; and second, we must be wrapped up in the life of our nation.

In order to collaborate with God, we must understand how God thinks. A study of His Word, of His actions and of His heart reveals the following:

- God loves nations.
- God wants to see nations repent and turn to Him.
- God has built into the nature of a woman all that it takes to ensure the preservation of her seed. In so doing, a woman collaborates with God and her nation benefits.
- The life of a great man or woman is wrapped up in the life of his or her nation.

This latter revelation came with the singing of a little chorus, "Hear my cry, Oh God, attend unto my prayer. From the end of the earth will I cry unto thee...."

In this Psalm (Psalm 62:1,2), David was weeping in the pain of intercession. But what seemed like a self-centered prayer was, upon closer examination, a man's cry for his entire nation. So let us not be selfish. Our identity is intricately bound up in God's purposes for our nations.

God is looking for collaborators. He seeks intercessors, prophets and priests whose hearts are big enough to accommodate nations within their care. The Father God, in His master design for the salvation of the world, provided His own Son, the Firstborn, to make atonement for the world He so loved. This same God has also designed that parents give themselves to their families and nations in intercession and so collaborate with Him in the salvation of those nations.

As parents, we should desire to achieve our purpose...this purpose, that our sons and daughters would be delivered and that our nations would be restored to righteousness. But we must see our lives as wrapped up in the life of the nation in which God has placed us as parents, as life givers, as intercessors and as collaborators with Him.

In our struggle for our nations, and in our efforts to move out of our particular situations of brokenness or loss, God is saying to us, "Women, I am giving to you the opportunity of your lives. Invest yourselves and your prayers and intercessions in the nations, and I will make you great. This is my promise to you."

It is a fight for life — for us and for our children. Hear the prophetic and urgent call. "I call heaven and earth to record this day against you, that I have set before you life and death, blessing and cursing: therefore choose life, *that both thou and thy seed* may live" (Deuteronomy 30:19).

2
War Breaks Out In The Garden — Enmity Established

And I will put enmity between thee and the woman, and between thy seed and her seed; it shall bruise thy head, and thou shalt bruise his heel.

Genesis 3:15

Adam must have relived that scene every day of his life. He could still see them ... the perfect form of his wife, Eve, her frown showing frustration for the first time in the history of the earth ... the sullen form of the serpent standing and hissing before the steady gaze of the Bright One, the Creator. The Master spoke of a battle between seed. What could He mean?

God saves nations through succeeding generations of righteous seed. By reproducing righteous seed in our families, we may literally ensure the restoration of our nations.

If a man wants to ensure his posterity, he must have a righteous seed. Likewise, if a nation wants to ensure its posterity, it must have righteous seed. There must be born into the nation a new generation with a heritage of godliness and the fear of the Lord.

If we are going to be involved in nation building, then we must be sure that the seed we produce is good, solid, and righteous. God planted a kingdom of righteousness right in the middle of the kingdom of darkness. He is establishing that kingdom.

9

He has ordained that our seed become His seed, the fruits of His Son, literally the Seed of Christ in the earth! In this way, even our mighty God ensures His posterity in the earth through OUR righteous seed!

God told Abraham, ''. . . in thee shall all families of the earth be blessed'' (Genesis 12:3). Another way to say this is: ''. . . in *your seed* all nations will be blessed.'' God is an eternal God who gives eternal promises, but His promises are guaranteed fulfillment only as succeeding generations appropriate those promised blessings.

When, in the past, I read genealogies recorded in the Bible, I could not understand why God would include them all. But I now believe that they are listed because all of the promises God gave to mankind have been, or shall be, fulfilled through the seed of Adam and his children.

God told Abraham, Isaac, Jacob, and Noah, that He would bless their seed. He would bless their nation through their seed. As I began to understand that God works through our seed, I was excited to discover how carefully He traces seed in His Word — both righteous and unrighteous seed.

Our eternal God spoke an eternal Word to righteous men and women who, in turn, were trusted to reproduce seed who would reproduce other generations of godly seed who would inherit the covenant and promised blessings spoken.

The Seed Of The Woman — Enmity Established

God preordained the birth of His Righteous Seed in a mysterious plan to enter the earth as the Seed of a woman. That Seed would ultimately dominate and destroy Satan. That declaration of enmity and war was made to Satan in Genesis 3:15:

And I will put enmity between thee and the woman, and between thy seed and her seed; it shall bruise thy head, and thou shalt bruise his heel.

God was in effect promising Eve, "I will put enmity between your seed and the seed of Satan. I am establishing enmity between your seed, Eve, and that which is against me (that of the enemy), and I am guaranteeing that your seed will crush the head of the enemy."

That word *enmity* means "hatred." It does not refer to casual dislike. It is used to describe intense, active, growing hostility. That's the way the devil feels about you and your seed, and that is the way we *should* feel about the devil and all of his works.

Listen, the same war that started in the terrible moment after the fall of Adam and Eve has spread into your home. It is very important for you and me to be prepared, to know how to fight our ancient enemy with God's weapons and win! Always remember this: the devil absolutely hates, loathes and despises you and your children. But he is powerless against alert, skilled warriors who know the power in the Name of Jesus and His Word!

Here then is the purpose of God through women in childbearing revealed: their righteous seed will forever crush the head of Satan's seed. You have God's Word! In Genesis 3:15, He uttered perhaps the greatest promise ever made. It is indeed a promise made by God to all women for the benefit of all mankind. But it is a promise which we must appropriate for our own children.

The Principle of Equivalent Effect

I have discovered the "Principle of Equivalent Effect" in the Word that was spoken to Eve. The Principle of Equivalent Effect is based on the unchanging nature of God. It states that every believer can and should experience the same effect the Word had on the original hearers who first received the Word. The Word of God is like that.

The effect the Word had on Eve must have had the same effect on Mary, the mother of Jesus, whose seed was to bruise the head of Satan. It must draw the same faith response from me, "...Be it unto me according to thy word..." (Luke 1:38). It is a principle.

As women say "yes" to God in faith, the Principle of Equivalent Effect begins to operate. Our obedience releases the power and wisdom of God, and we release the potential of our seed to conquer Satan and his designs.

We are in a warfare. We have a big enemy and that enemy is Satan. The moment we forget that, we are in trouble, because from morning until night, we are involved in a battle.

Before a woman even conceives, the enemy is after her seed. Satan wants to rule and dominate our children. His ultimate aim is to destroy them. They represent the greatest threat to his evil works in the decades before Jesus' return!

So we must fight continually for the lives of our children (and our husbands), because our seed is guaranteed, in Christ, to bruise the head of Satan in their generation.

We do not have to fear. The Psalmist enjoins us to "...fear no evil..." (Psalm 23:4). He again proclaimed, "The Lord is my light and my salvation; whom shall I fear? the Lord is the strength of my life; of whom shall I be afraid?" (Psalm 27:1). We must be strong, and we must fight a good fight for the survival of our family members.

Parents, as we fight in the Spirit to preserve our families, our nations will be saved. The survival of your nation depends on the survival of your seed and of a new generation which has complete loyalty and obedience to God.

The Principle of Generational Promises

Another principle that applies to us today is closely related to the Principle of Equivalent Effect. It is the Principle of Generational Promises. Both principles underscore the eternal nature of God and the image of eternity which is stamped upon God's creation, man. Inherent within it is the intriguing reality of man's partnership with God.

God is a generational God, whose promises to a specific man or woman are often to be fulfilled in their succeeding generations or in His descendants. It may happen hundreds of years later as in the birth of Jesus in David's lineage, centuries after David's death.

God said to Abraham:

> **For I know him, that he will command his children and his household after him, and they shall keep the way of the Lord, to do justice and judgment; that the Lord may bring upon Abraham that which he hath spoken of him.**
>
> **Genesis 18:19**

God chose to make a covenant with Abraham, a man who would ensure that His divine Word, eternal in its nature, would be fulfilled through His righteous seed.

Many or all of God's promises to us come to fruition as we train our children to obey God's law, as our children develop obedience to our righteous guidance, and as we teach God's promises to our children. Then, with anticipation, faith, and a sense of purpose and destiny, they inherit the promises. A promise is not always simply something for us to experience now. But it is always something for our children to inherit, and ultimately, for our nation to live by.

Nine generations before Abraham, God promised Noah, "... behold, I establish my covenant with you, and with your seed after you" (Genesis 9:9). The covenant was to be fulfilled through righteous Noah, who was himself

13

able "to command his children and his household after him" (Genesis 18:19).

God's promises are for you and your seed. Why? Because through our seed "the way of the Lord" (Genesis 18:19) will be preserved. He will save the nations through our seed. How? Godly children grow up to fearlessly preach the Gospel and turn their nations to God. God guarantees the building of His kingdom, but He is vitally interested in righteous seed, for they are His divinely anointed and appointed kingdom builders.

Seth was a prototype of "righteous" seed. After Cain killed Abel, God gave Adam and Eve another seed, a son whom they named Seth.

> **And Adam knew his wife again; and she bare a son, and called his name Seth: For God, said she, hath appointed me another seed instead of Abel, whom Cain slew.**
>
> **And to Seth, to him also there was born a son; and he called his name Enos: then began men to call upon the name of the Lord.**
>
> **Genesis 4:25,26**

God guaranteed the fulfillment of His Genesis 3:15 promise by giving Eve another son. Seth lived a full life, so the propagation of seed continued. He inherited the blessing of Genesis 1:28, and God's plan for succeeding generations of children of purpose and destiny began its steady course.

Do You Think The Way God Does?

We tend to look at things with our physical eyes, but God wants us to look at things through our spiritual eyes, to see people and circumstances as He sees them.

In Genesis 5:6-10, God carefully records Adam's generations:

- And Seth lived an hundred and five years, and begat Enos:
- And Seth lived after he begat Enos eight hundred and seven years, and he begat sons and daughters:
- And Enos lived ninety years, and begat Cainan:
- And Enos lived after he begat Cainan eight hundred and fifteen years, and begat sons and daughters.

Have you noticed how God, the Holy Spirit, directed the written account of Seth's lineage or posterity? It appears that God considers a person's total age to include the years before the seed arrived, plus the years after the seed came. Both of these added together equal total life span.

God is interested in seed. He sees us from the point of view of seed and of reproducing seed, because He has made a promise. He put enmity between the woman and the seed of Satan, and He guarantees that we, in Christ, shall crush the seed of the enemy. Our seed must do it. This is the way God looks at life. The generational promise is for the seed, made righteous through Christ, to live overcoming lives, crushing the head and kingdom of Satan.

The Principle of Prophetic Intention

One of the greatest benefits of serving our faithful God is that every prophetic word He speaks to us releases also the certain potential for its fulfillment (if we do our part).

The Principle of Prophetic Intention identifies the truth that every prophetic word spoken by God contains within that word all of the necessary ingredients to fulfill that word. This law adds a future dimension to all of God's actions as they pertain to His spoken intention.

It is God's plan to raise up men and women who will deliver nations. God appears always to be thinking a generation ahead of us. So when He is ready to deliver a nation, He begins to prepare the deliverer from the mother's womb! God's purpose for that child is to fulfill His prophetic purpose. The seed embodies the prophetic intention of God to raise up deliverers.

In Judges 13, we read about Samson's mother. At the time of Samson's conception, there was evil in the land, and the land was under judgment. ''And the children of Israel did evil again in the sight of the Lord; and the Lord delivered them into the hand of the Philistines (the enemy) forty years'' (Judges 13:1).

Then God gave the woman who was to be Samson's mother a promise. It was a promise with a potential for the deliverance of Israel.

> And there was a certain man of Zorah, of the family of the Danites, whose name was Manoah; and his wife was barren, and bare not.
>
> And the angel of the Lord appeared unto the woman, and said unto her, Behold now, thou art barren, and bearest not: but thou shalt conceive, and bear a son.
>
> Now therefore beware, I pray thee, and drink not wine nor strong drink, and eat not any unclean thing:
>
> For, lo, thou shalt conceive, and bear a son; and no razor shall come on his head: for the child shall be a Nazarite unto God from the womb: *and he shall begin to deliver Israel out of the hand of the Philistines.*
>
> Judges 13:2-5

God wants to bless our children with the ability to deliver nations. You may be saying, ''But not my child. God isn't talking about my child.'' The truth is that every young life that is born has the potential for delivering a nation. If your children do not begin to deliver your nation, it may be that you have not taught them how to do it, or heeded the heart cry and search of God for righteous seed. Or, it may be that you have not blessed your children and released the potential within them for delivering your nation.

Great poets have developed a rich repertoire of words, and the ability to use them lavishly and creatively. In a sense, these "masters of words" just kept on doing what their peers stopped doing!

The spoken and written Word is a God-given, creative tool. A child in the crib will babble and coo contentedly for hours. A child using his God-given gift of speech is a natural talker and a creative person. If that gift is nurtured and given release, practice and exposure, it will form the foundation for the fulfillment of your child's eternally-ordained purpose in God.

Your children can deliver a nation if they keep on doing what is natural for them to do. Remember, your child was born with nation building in his spirit. He was born a person of authority. God told Adam and Eve (and thus their descendants) to have dominion in Genesis 1:27,28; yet, sometimes we bring our children up as frightened weaklings. When this innate potential for leadership and for confident rulership receives our blessing and encouragement, it releases a free flow of divine empowerment God put in them before their conception.

As mothers, we must say to our children, "God has given you to me to train you to become a Samson, a Joseph, a Moses, or an Esther in our nation." Then we must work for it day and night. A prophecy will not simply happen just because a prophetic word of promise came from God one time, like it did to Samson's mother. She received a dramatic word from an angel, "...and he shall begin to deliver Israel out of the hand of the Philistines" (Judges 13:5).

God didn't simply drop a full-grown Samson into her lap. He required some difficult tasks of her. If your child becomes a nation builder, it will happen because day and night, you as a parent live it and you speak it forth.

Godly parents are called in this day — as they were in the times of Moses, Samson, John the Baptist and Jesus Christ — to build the nations in which God has placed them, as they diligently and patiently train their children in the way of truth and righteousness.

Do you want a higher call than the one you now have? It is the one you have always had — Nation Building! You are called to deliver your nation, whether it is the United States, Germany, Jamaica, the Bahamas, Japan or the Soviet Union!

Tomorrow's spiritual, moral and social revival will not come from the politicians. It will come from our righteous seed who commit themselves to secure spiritual and social change and restoration using Biblical principles. And so it was since the beginning of time.

God said to Abraham, "...In thee (your seed) shall all families (nations) of the earth be blessed" (Genesis 12:3).

The Principle of Reproduction

When God chooses us as parents, and gives us His promises for our children, He actually intends for us to reproduce ourselves in our children.

As God gives us children, He will give us prophetic words to speak over them. We must speak forth God's Word upon their lives, pray for them, and remind them of it. The confessed Word, and the teaching and lifestyle we encourage all cause the seed to take root and to develop into the full promise of God for their lives.

I speak God's Word over my children, I pray it, and I live it every day. Sometimes I'm tired at night, but before I go to bed, I walk around my children's beds and pray and talk to them. Or when I am driving, I ask my children, "What do you think of _____? One day you also will also become a _____." I speak life and encouragement over my children because I am determined to have righteous seed. I believe I am reproducing myself and all of God's promises in my children.

The Bible declares that everything created by God was given power and potential to reproduce its own kind (Genesis 1:11-25).

The first law of nature, divinely declared, is that of reproduction. Plants reproduce after their own kind. Animals reproduce after their own kind. It is this first creative eternal law of Genesis which empowers and constrains godly parents to reproduce godly offspring. God has divinely placed this urge within parents. It is through us that He expresses His divine desire to train deliverers of nations. So why should I not reproduce after my own kind?

When I declared that my three sons and my daughter all have a higher call to be ministers of the Gospel, I was accused of being selfish. The accusers were humanist and secularist. They had no vision for the building of godly nations. From my viewpoint, their view of life, the world, and our purpose on earth is a form of narrow-minded tunnel vision.

The very law which predetermines my children's color or hair texture also authorizes and obligates me to reproduce my spiritual attributes! Spiritual endowment is just as real and natural as is genetic endowment. When we are born again, Jesus places His divine genes of immortality and righteousness within us to pass on to our children.

I was born into a large family, with four brothers and four sisters. Each of my siblings is now reproducing after his or her own kind. Each is now producing a particular lifestyle for his or her family, and children with peculiar tastes for food or music, and so on.

I graduated from a university with people who are now accountants. The major themes of their family discussions are accounts and business. They are reproducing accountants. This exemplifies the law of reproduction.

In my home, with a pastor for a husband and father, we discuss and live the ministry of the Gospel. A lifestyle of godly living will produce children who are "trained in the way they should go" (Proverbs 22:6). I am reproducing after my own kind.

We all need to live righteous lives and reproduce righteous seed after our own kind. Our righteous seed will then participate in the deliverance and rebuilding of our nations. They will become the future ministers of the Gospel, Christian teachers, professionals and craftsmen, godly politicians and athletes!

If we sow national awareness, godly principles and a love for God's rulership within our children, we will reap seed who will establish the kingdom of God in our nation.

3
Jeremiah — An Example Of
A Pre-Ordained Deliverer

Listen, O isles, unto me; and hearken, ye people, from far; The Lord hath called me from the womb; from the bowels of my mother hath he made mention of my name.

And he hath made my mouth like a sharp sword; in the shadow of his hand hath he hid me, and made me a polished shaft; in his quiver hath he hid me;

And said unto me, Thou art my servant, O Israel, in whom I will be glorified.

Isaiah 49:1-3

Hilkiah was an ordinary priest of Anathoth. He named his son, Jeremiah, which means "The Lord is exalted" or "The Lord hurls Himself like an arrow." It is not difficult to imagine that Jeremiah's parents trained him to live out his name.Jeremiah grew up to become a fearless prophet of Jehovah. God had given a promise before Jeremiah was biologically or spiritually shaped. God's plan for Jeremiah had to do with saving a nation. His plan had to do with world affairs.

It appears that not only was the divine law of reproduction set in motion even before Jeremiah's conception, but God Himself had intervened to provide for the nation a prophet/deliverer. The prophet describes God's words to him in Jeremiah 1:5.

Before I *formed* thee in the belly I *knew* thee; and before thou camest forth out of the womb I *sanctified*

21

thee, and I *ordained* thee a prophet unto the nations.

This statement reveals God's strategy for every generation and nation: **God supernaturally intervenes long before the conception of our children and pre-programs His own purposes into their lives.**

First of all, understand that Jeremiah's name meant something. Sometimes we give our children names without giving thought to the meaning of those names. In extreme cases, parents may need to consider a name change for one of their children.

One friend of mine changed her daughter's name from the questionable "Natanja" to "Naomi" (my pleasant one). Another changed her son's name from "Damian" (which in some languages and dialects means "demon or devil") to "Christian."

Secondly, the Bible records God's practice of setting His chosen men and women apart unto Himself from birth. This was the case with Samson (Judges 13:2-25), Samuel (1 Samuel 1:17-19,27, 28), John the Baptist (Luke 1:15-17), Jesus Christ (Matthew 1:18-25) and Paul (Galatians 1:15,16).

When we begin to think in the same way in which our generational, eternal, and covenant-making God thinks, it becomes evident that God still continues to place His divine hope within the implanted seed of the woman. For each one of these precious ones, it is His hope that they will become a nation builder and a deliverer for their generation.

Each of our children has been spiritually shaped and given a divine purpose by the Creator. God told Jeremiah and many others who would follow, "I sanctified thee." To sanctify means "to set apart or to be on God's side." There are only two possible sides. The other is that of the enemy of our seed, Satan, with whom there is established an eternal enmity. There is a relentless battle going on —

our seed versus the enemy, Satan, who wants our children on his side!

Thirdly, Jeremiah was sanctified for the sake of God's Kingdom. He was set aside or separated to be on God's side. "... I sanctified thee, and I ordained thee a prophet unto the nations" (Jeremiah 1:5).

Jeremiah was a prophet, appointed to prophesy against Judah and against its religious and national leaders (Verse 18). The entire book of Jeremiah is an account of how he lived out his name, fearlessly proclaiming the sanctions of a holy God, even though his unpopular words put his life in danger.

I believe that this is exactly what is needed in our nations across the Caribbean and the world today. Jeremiah preached against vanity. He lashed out against sin in the land. He preached fearlessly and relentlessly against prophet, priest and wise man. He said that they were not at all ashamed of the abominations they had committed.

> Were they ashamed when they had committed abomination? nay, they were not at all ashamed, neither could they blush: therefore they shall fall among them that fall: at the time that I visit them they shall be cast down, saith the Lord.
>
> Jeremiah 6:15

The theme of Jeremiah is found in chapter 7, verses 8 and 9. It is a cry against national iniquity and idolatry.

> Behold, ye trust in lying words, that cannot profit.
>
> Will ye steal, murder, and commit adultery, and swear falsely, and burn incense unto Baal, and walk after other gods whom ye know not?

Jeremiah dedicated his life to the deliverance of his nation. Again and again he confronted the people with their sin and warned of consequences and God's judgment.

In 1988, Jamaica was devastated by Hurricane Gilbert. There was one area in particular that was very hard hit. It was to be the site of a major cult celebration dealing with the occult and ancestral spirits. They practice openly in Jamaica. Certain people in high places agreed for this celebration to take place and planned for it. I believe the site for that planned celebration was wiped out by God's hand in the hurricane winds!

My heart breaks whenever I read in Jeremiah 7:18 that little children were involved in the abominations by their parents. I believe God raised up Jeremiah to deliver the children.

> The children gather wood, and the fathers kindle the fire, and the women knead their dough to make cakes to the queen of heaven, and to pour out drink offerings unto other gods, that they may provoke me to anger.

Not only are we as parents indulging in various types of idolatry, but in addition, we have our children "carrying the wood." Fathers and husbands "kindle the fire" while mothers and wives "knead their dough." We wield much influence, not only upon our children, but also upon our spouses. The ball is on our side of the court, women. We have a great influence in our homes, yet this is what happens when we not only practice ungodliness but also involve the entire family in it.

"To the queen of heaven" refers to idolatrous worship. I want you to notice that *the children were involved*. The people of Judah had their seed, who are supposed to be righteous, involved in worship of the queen of heaven. But the sin even went beyond that! The people also plotted against Jeremiah.

> Then said they, Come, and let us devise devices against Jeremiah; for the law shall not perish from the priest, nor counsel from the wise, nor the word from

the prophet. Come, and let us smite him with the
tongue, and let us not give heed to any of his words.
Jeremiah 18:18

Prophet, priest and king in that nation were plotting
against Jeremiah, because he spoke the truth as he warned
them of God's wrath. As priests of the Lord, we may declare
God's judgments and be persecuted for it. However, if we
do not speak the truth and continue to warn the people,
then the judgment proclaimed by Jeremiah — the inevitable
result of hard-hearted rebellion — would be the fate of our
nations. Jeremiah 18:21 proclaimed that fate.

> Therefore deliver up their children to the famine,
> and pour out their blood by the force of the sword; and
> let their wives be bereaved of their children, and be
> widows; and let their men be put to death; let their
> young men be slain by the sword in battle.

Let us notice and be warned that the central recipient
of that judgment is the family. The pain of judgment brings
grief to every member of the family.

God's hand has not yet lifted from the Caribbean
Islands. A prophetic word warned that within a few months
of the 1988 hurricane, we would see much pain, perhaps
even famine in our nations. God hates our sin. Just as God
raised up Jeremiah in his day, so He has given us righteous
seed to be raised up in this hour.

When my son, Christopher, was born, his father said
of him, "He has such a fierce spirit." Today, it is this same
spirit which causes Christopher to speak out. He hates
injustice. If I make the slightest unjust move, he says,
"Mommy, you shouldn't have done that." He sees clearly
and militates against perceived injustice of any kind. He is
fierce and he does have a fighting spirit. He is sanctified
and "separated" to be a minister of God, and God is going
to use that same spirit to speak His Word to law-breaking
nations.

Mothers, we are not to quench our children's natural strengths unless they are misused for evil intention. God wants to use those strong qualities in our children, if they are supportive of His plans and purposes.

I have another son who tends to be quiet. However, when he opens his mouth, pure and undiluted wisdom comes out. So I do not force him to speak. I let him wait. Then when we want an answer, we may say, "What do you think?" and he opens his mouth with a word which contains the essence of all the Biblical knowledge, understanding and wisdom which he has been taught.

We must not quench the gifts of the children. We must use our God-given discernment and parental wisdom to know how to direct our children in their growth. We dare not curb or silence the very qualities that God has implanted in our children to save our nations!

One time, in my eagerness to see my sons attain their higher calling as ministers, I said to one of them (after watching a popular minister preach), "Would you like to preach like So-and-so?"

I thought I was training my son so well. Then that preacher I'd placed my son's eye on fell because of sin. The world knew about the sin, and my son, of course, knew about it, too. I said to myself, "My God, what did I plant in his heart?"

I had to repent. God has forbidden us to find idols in the world. He does not even want us to find idols in the Bible. Examples of God's grace at work in imperfect people, yes. Idols, no.

For instance, Moses murdered, David committed adultery and Peter blasphemed. We are not to point to a man as the measure of perfection. We must point to Jesus Christ alone. Only He can be the example for our righteous seed.

4
Parenting With A Purpose

For unto us a child is born, unto us a son is given: and the government shall be upon his shoulder: and his name shall be called Wonderful, Counsellor, The mighty God, The everlasting Father, The Prince of Peace.

Of the increase of his government and peace there shall be no end, upon the throne of David, and upon his kingdom, to order it, and to establish it with judgment and with justice from henceforth even for ever. The zeal of the Lord of hosts will perform this.

Isaiah 9:6,7

God's first blessing in Eden gave Adam and Eve the ability to reproduce life. And to Eve, God gave the potential to preserve life through His promise of redemption and the removal of the curse (See Genesis 3:15 and Romans 8:18-23).

From the creation of Eve to her descendants today, **women are life-givers.** In our tongue is the law of life (Proverbs 3:1,2). The law of the Spirit of life abides in us (Romans 8:2). We generate life. Our hands touch and give life. Our mouths speak life to our children. Through God, we are well equipped to win our battle with the enemy.

The Little Girl I Had Scorned

Years ago, I had a vision in which I was running as fast as I could up a street in San Fernando, my hometown in Trinidad. A little girl of about two years of age was running behind me. Her skin was encrusted with dirt and muck, and her hair was tangled with dirt. I was running from this

27

little girl because I scorned her. I did not want her to touch me.

Then the scene changed. When I looked again, I had this child in my arms. I played sweet music for her even though she was deaf. And as I played, her hearing was restored. I touched her tenderly and everywhere I touched her became clean and sweet. I had so much to share with this little girl, and it was so easy for me to make her clean and sweet.

The scene changed again. I saw the little girl now grown, dressed and painted like a prostitute, a 'lady of the night.' She was pursuing me in anger, bent on revenge. She was venting her anger towards me because I had deserted her when I outran her tired, dirty little feet. She was the little girl I had scorned.

When I looked again, God showed me that the little girl — and the woman — was me, but for His grace!!

Through that unforgettable vision, God gave me a burden for forsaken children everywhere. We must reach out to the young. We have so much of the Word, so much life in us. We must touch, redeem and restore God's precious heritage by our hands and words.

This call is for single as well as married believers. Do not become absorbed in a life of loneliness. Share your life with a little needy child. Many couples and single people in our church in Kingston, Jamaica, have adopted children or provided foster homes for them.

One time, there was an infant boy in the hospital who was found, malnourished and dying, after being abandoned for days. A couple took him into their home, even though they already had two babies of their own, and their entire family caught scabies from him! Was that too high a price to pay?

Please do not say to me, "I have my own children." That precious child has since been adopted by a Christian couple, and God's hand is clearly upon his life. One day he will be a minister of the Gospel, just as God gave the prophetic word to his adoptive mother!

Satan, our enemy, has not relented in his strategy to hook and trap our righteous seed. He hasn't even bothered to be subtle. Look at all the innocent children who are abandoned, malnourished, delinquent or even incarcerated. Satan is after the seed. How does he further his plan? He often tries to bring in ungodly people to adopt or foster them.

These defenseless children, already suffering from an orphan spirit, rejection from the womb, and diseases stemming from neglect, are thrown into homes where adults do not know God. They often become the objects of emotional, physical and sexual abuse.

One night I was flat on my back, under the power of the Holy Spirit, when the Lord spoke to me, "I want you to speak out on behalf of these children and do something about their plight."

As you read these words, I must obey the Lord and urgently encourage you: **Enlarge your tents, extend your borders, reproduce yourself and nurture a fatherless, orphan child.** Women, whether you are married or single, your hands are for giving and sharing life, and for raising up righteous seed.

Parenting With a Purpose

The chief purpose of parenting is to fulfill God's mission and raise up our children to hear and honor God's voice.

God's purpose for giving us righteous seed who will bring healing and deliverance to the nations is clearly outlined in His Word.

The success our children have in the fulfillment of their God-given mission depends to a great extent on the level of our dedication as nurturing parents or guardians.

We should meet several conditions as God-appointed care-givers and teachers:

1. Every parent should know the prophetic word or plan of God for his or her newborn, and should be aware of the history and circumstances surrounding the promise.

2. That word should be clearly spoken to the child at appropriate times.

3. Every other 'significant' care-giver should be made aware of God's call on the life of the child.

4. Every plan, activity, or teaching undertaken by nurturers on behalf of the child should be with the awareness of the child's call and mission. Each child's life is to be a preparation for that call and teachers and care-givers are to collaborate and work together with God towards that goal.

5. Parents have the sole responsibility to see to it that the God-given purpose for their children is faithfully worked out by all collaborating teachers and nurturers. It must be a "team" approach.

6. Preparations must include structured discipleship for spiritual growth, educational programs for intellectual and academic development, and all other social, moral, and physical training necessary for the nurturing of the righteous seed.

7. The goals of the whole life program must be knowing Christ, having a Christ-like character, acquiring a knowledge of God's purpose for each life, developing the skills and wisdom needed to fulfill that purpose, and pursuing a determined vocational direction and apprenticeship program.

The Bible gives us three outstanding examples of parents who helped their righteous seed fulfill their mission. These should encourage us.

Mission Fulfilled — Hannah and Samuel

During one of the darkest periods in Israel's history, a childless woman asked God for a child. In her fervent prayer, she vowed to return the child to God if He would hear her cry and redeem her from the curse of a barren womb. God set into motion a miracle that would grant her request as well as provide Israel with a leader who would gloriously raise it to new heights as a nation.

After Samuel's miraculous birth, his parents carefully and methodically obeyed the Lord's requirement that he be raised as a Nazarite given to God's service (I Samuel 1, 2:1-21). Their parenting was marked by purpose and constant awareness of the destiny of their young son. Hannah and Elkanah weaned Samuel and promptly arranged for his delivery to Eli the priest for training and discipleship as a servant in the temple.

Every year, Hannah made an ephod (a symbol of priestly service and consecration) for her son and faithfully carried out her part of Samuel's preparation for ministry as judge and prophet of Israel.Samuel made steady progress under Eli's supervision:

I Samuel 2:11	"...And the child did minister unto the Lord before Eli the priest."
I Samuel 2:21	"...And the child Samuel grew before the Lord."
I Samuel 3:1	"And the child Samuel ministered unto the Lord before Eli...."
I Samuel 3:19-21	"And Samuel grew, and the Lord was with him, and did let none of his words fall to the ground.

"And all Israel...knew that Samuel was established to be a prophet of the Lord.

"...For the Lord revealed Himself to Samuel...."

I Samuel 4:1   "And the word of Samuel came to all Israel...."

The birth of Samuel marks one of God's most remarkable works, where He matched the earnest need and vow of a barren and heartbroken woman with the desperate need of Israel. God took that faithful vow and Eli's work of preparation together with Samuel's willingness, and brought forth a powerful judge of Israel. And God will do it again!

Mission Fulfilled —
Elisabeth and John the Baptist

God's ancient promise to send a Deliverer and Messiah to Israel was tied to another promise of righteous seed. John the Baptist was destined to be the forerunner of the Messiah (Matthew 11:10-14; Luke 7:27-29).

Did John's parents collaborate with God? Luke 1:5-7 records the history of John's elderly parents, an ordinary priest named Zacharias, and his barren wife Elisabeth. They were a righteous couple "...walking in all the commandments and ordinances of the Lord blameless" (Luke 1:6). They had, no doubt, followed the history of their people and looked forward to the birth of the promised Messiah.

When God spoke to Zacharias in the Holy of Holies through His heralding angel, the prophetic word was clear, detailed and specific:

...and thy wife Elisabeth shall bear thee a son, and thou shalt call his name John.

> ...He shall be great in the sight of the Lord ...
> He shall be filled with the Holy Ghost, even from his
> mother's womb.
>
> And many of the children of Israel shall he turn
> to the Lord their God.
>
> And he shall go before him in the spirit and power
> of Elias, to turn the hearts of the fathers to the children,
> and the disobedient to the wisdom of the just; to make
> ready a people prepared for the Lord.
>
> Luke 1:13-17

Zacharias heard the word, understood it, believed it and began acting upon it. How did Elisabeth collaborate with God in the nurturing and training of John? She not only obeyed God in the training of her own seed, but she also ministered to the mother of the Messiah through the Holy Ghost!

When Mary first entered Elisabeth's house, little John leaped in his mother's womb in supernatural recognition of the Holy Seed in Mary's womb. In Luke 1:45, Elisabeth spoke a powerful word of confirmation and encouragement to Mary, "And blessed is she that believed: *for there shall be a performance of those things which were told her from the Lord.*"

By the time John was born, Elisabeth's neighbors and cousins all knew of God's promise for him. This mother was faithful to proclaim the Word of the Lord over her unborn seed, and to all who would touch and influence him.

On the eighth day after John's birth, the neighbors tried to give Elisabeth's baby the name of his father after common Jewish custom, but his parents insisted, "...Not so; but he shall be called John" (Luke 1:60), as the angel had stated.

John means "the Grace of Jehovah." By obeying the wishes of God, John's parents blessed their child with a supernatural and prophetic name and invoked into his life the potential and ability to fulfill the prophetic promise spoken concerning him.

The prophetic words of Zacharias (Luke 1:67-79) expressed God's hope and "statement of intention" for John's life and ministry. Zacharias dedicated his life to a divine purpose — the bringing up of a seed with a divinely-ordained mission.

Though his ministry was brief, John the Baptist was called "the greatest of all the prophets" by Jesus Christ (See Matthew 11:9-11).

Mission Fulfilled — Mary and Jesus Christ

What greater example of supernatural parenting and nation-building seed can be found than the mother of the child who was to become the chief agent in the "Battle of the Seed"?

Jesus Christ, the Seed of woman, was promised to the world in the Garden of Eden. He was the Seed that crushed the head of Satan (See Genesis 3:15).

Mary, the mother of Jesus, was an ordinary, devout and pure virgin. Growing up in a Jewish home, Mary had heard the Scriptures recited in her home concerning the coming Messiah.

She probably shared the same secret hope in her heart that thousands of Jewish girls had dreamed before her, the secret dream that she would be the one chosen to bear the Seed.

Joseph, Mary's espoused husband-to-be, was a common carpenter. He was also chosen and prepared by God for his supernatural parenting task. He had some solid religious training as well as a Davidic lineage and ancestry. He would be the one to raise and educate Jesus, the King of the Jews and Savior of the world!

Matthew carefully recorded that lineage in Matthew 1:1-16. This bloodline accurately details God's meticulous fulfillment of prophecy and promise from Abraham, through David, to the birth of the Messiah — exactly as God promised.

The generational line runs from Abraham to Jesse, to David, to Jacob, who was the father of "Joseph, the husband of Mary, of whom was born Jesus, who is called Christ" (Verse 16). Jesus was the Son of Abraham *and* of David by direct descent (See Luke 1:2-16 and Romans 9:5).

While Matthew traced the line through the lineage of Joseph, Luke traced David's line through Heli, the father of Mary (Luke 3:23-38). It is interesting that God carefully planned that the heritage of Jesus could be traced back through both Joseph and Mary. God is indeed a generational God.

These detailed genealogical records clearly underscore God's intricate and patient outworking of His promise through 41 generations! Mary and Joseph were chosen to nurture, raise and instruct the Divine Seed who would crush the head of the serpent!

Children Are Blessings, Not Accidents

Jesus Christ, conceived of the Holy Spirit in the womb of an unmarried virgin, was the divine fulfillment of ancient promises made to two of Israel's most famous leaders, Abraham and King David.

God's promise to Abraham in Genesis 12:1-3, "In thee shall all the families of the earth be blessed," was fulfilled through his direct descendant, Jesus Christ.

The virgin Mary also received a promise in Luke 1:31-33:

...**Thou shalt bring forth a son, and shalt call his name JESUS.**

He shall be great, and shall be called the Son of the Highest: and the Lord God shall give unto him the throne of his father David:

And he shall reign over the house of Jacob for ever; and of his kingdom there shall be no end.

Elisabeth prophesied to Mary about the child in her womb, "...blessed is the fruit of thy womb" (Luke 1:42).

Mary responded under the inspiration of the Holy Spirit, delivering in the spontaneous praise and prophetic song of the Magnificat, God's divine intention for the Seed in Luke 1:46-55.

Mary drew on her solid Jewish training under the leading of God's Spirit. She recalled the promises spoken throughout the history of her people:

He hath holpen his servant Israel, in remembrance of his mercy;

As he spake to our fathers, to Abraham, *and to his seed forever.*

Luke 1:54,55

Can you see how important it is to remember every prophetic word spoken for our seed? Even the parents of Jesus Christ and John the Baptist were careful to observe this fact. The scriptures underscore this again and again.

Not only did Mary remember the prophetic word and believe the word of the angel and of Elisabeth, but she pondered all those things in her heart and prepared to bring up the child Jesus to inherit God's promises and so to fulfill His mission.

Luke 2:40 says, "And the child grew and waxed strong in spirit, filled with wisdom: and the grace of God was upon him." Luke 2:52 further states, "And Jesus increased in wisdom and stature, and in favor with God and man." Jesus Himself knew His mission. He had been carefully educated and groomed for it by His parents. In the temple, with confidence and a spirit of purpose and destiny, He loudly proclaimed it. "The spirit of the Lord is upon me...to preach the gospel to the poor...to preach the acceptable year of the Lord" (Luke 4:18,19).

Jesus Christ, with the confidence that comes from faith in all of God's promises, and with a surety about the call on His life, made a public claim: "...This day is this scripture fulfilled in your ears" (Luke 4:21). Later, Jesus declared, "...I must preach the kingdom of God to other cities also: *for therefore am I sent*" (Verse 43).

The divine mission of the Seed of woman was backed by prophecy and history and fully accomplished by Jesus' birth, His self-proclaimed destiny, and sense of mission, His death, and His resurrection.

The Apostle Paul urged Timothy to remember the God-breathed prophecies spoken over him in I Timothy 1:18:

> **This charge I commit unto thee, son Timothy,** *according to the prophecies* **which went before on thee,** *that thou by them* **mightest war a good warfare.**

Not only will our seed grow up with their God-ordained call before them, but they will be able to "war a good warfare" by those prophecies as adult believers and ministers.

Inherent in this scripture is a powerful truth: the purposes of God, spoken to parents for their seed, become a powerful weapon of spiritual warfare. If God has given a purpose and promise, then He has provided everything necessary to fulfill that purpose. The end is already determined and set, so as parents, we simply have to "run the race"!

5

Teach A Child,
Establish A Foundation

> As for me, this is my covenant with them, saith
> the Lord; My spirit that is upon thee, and my words
> which I have put in thy mouth, shall not depart out
> of thy mouth, nor out of the mouth of thy seed, nor
> out of the mouth of thy seed's seed, saith the Lord,
> from henceforth and for ever.
>
> Isaiah 59:21

God makes it clear in His Word: we are to teach our children. Diligent teaching and training are the primary ways we can give our children a working knowledge of our Holy God, of His mighty acts and His ways. It is through our patient training and rehearsal of God's Word that our children can learn about His faithfulness and His encompassing greatness.

The Jewish people passed the truths of God on to their children orally from generation to generation, from parent to child.

Hasidic Jews still live in strict accordance with the Mosaic laws and the Pharisaic tradition. They still train their young men in the rabbinic tradition, discussing the scriptures and law around a table or circle.

In structured two-way conversation, using proverbs and direct quotes, the senior rabbi or teacher asks questions and drills his students about details of the written and oral traditions. The teacher may purposefully tell a story incorrectly or improperly quote a scripture to catch his students unaware, and to develop a keen sense of accuracy and detail in their minds.

Psalm 78 gives a quick, breathtaking and panoramic view of how the Jews transferred the knowledge of God throughout some five generations! It is God's divine plan that His Word, His law, His power and events portraying His faithfulness are poured down through His agents, parents and children and grandchildren. When we neglect this, we run the risk of bringing up rebellious and godless generations.

Give ear, O my people, to my law: incline your ears to the words of my mouth.

I will open my mouth in a parable: I will utter dark sayings of old:

Which we have heard and known, and our fathers have told us.

We will not hide them from their children, shewing to the generation to come the praises of the Lord, and his strength, and his wonderful works that he hath done.

For he established a testimony in Jacob, and appointed a law in Israel, which he commanded our fathers, that they should make them known to their children:

That the generation to come might know them, even the children which should be born; who should arise and declare them to their children:

That they might set their hope in God, and not forget the works of God, but keep his commandments:

And might not be as their fathers, a stubborn and rebellious generation; a generation that set not their heart aright, and whose spirit was not stedfast with God.

Psalm 78:1-8

There are seven reasons we should educate our children in God's ways. Every one of them appears in Psalm 78.

1. We will pass on the praises of God, His strength and His wonderful works (Verse 4).

2. Our righteous example will cause *our children* to arise and declare these things *to their children* (Verse 6).

3. It will cause our children to set their hope in the God of their fathers who has shown Himself faithful (Verse 7).

4. We teach them so that they will not forget God's works. (This is the reason we should use constant rehearsal and repetition, the same methods used to teach our children language and basic factual knowledge.) (Verse 7). Forgetfulness concerning God's covenant promises and judgments result in rebellion and national disobedience.

5. Solid training in God's Word encourages our children to keep His commandments (Verse 7).

6. Authoritative teaching and training in God's Word help steer our children away from the attitudes and sins of a stubborn and rebellious generation (Verse 8). A modern restatement of this is: "The generation without a knowledge of the mistakes of past history are doomed to repeat them."

7. Our children will honor the covenants of God if they are taught about them and their importance to their daily lives (Verse 10).

God has not changed. Parents are to rehearse God's Word to their children daily. Every morning and night they should learn about His faithfulness, His powerful hand in the affairs of history (for families and nations), and about His desire to work and be glorified through obedient and holy seed.

Parents Have A Mission From God

God has delegated the education of the children to parents. Christian schools and teachers may provide many services parents are unable to. Our children must be equipped with the best education available, whether it be in the spiritual, scientific, artistic, or literary areas.

However, we must never neglect to monitor WHAT our children are taught! This becomes even more important when we realize we are overseeing the education of children *who are being groomed to build nations and deliver their generations* through God's anointing!

Here are some helpful guidelines for parents and teachers who are charged with the vital task of training nation builders:

1. **Teach your children "to offer acceptable sacrifices to God."**

   God created us to offer up spiritual offerings of praise and thanksgiving to Him. He has always required that our sacrifices be acceptable.

   In Genesis 4:4, Abel offered acceptable sacrifices to God, but Cain's sacrifice was rejected. Cain and Abel were equally instructed about sacrifice, or God wouldn't have corrected Cain as He did. Cain failed to do what he knew was right. His willfulness turned to resentment and then to uncontrolled anger and jealousy, and he murdered his brother.

   Parents and teachers must teach belief in Jesus Christ as the atonement for sin and train children to curb or control their self-will. They should be taught to do only those things which please God. "Shaping" a child's will must begin early or parents will later endure much suffering as they watch self-willed children break God's law and suffer the inevitable consequences.

42

2. **Teach your children to hear and heed the voice of God (Genesis 5:8).**

   When God entered the garden of Eden and called for Adam and Eve after they had sinned, they hid themselves in fear from the familiar voice (Genesis 3:10).

   Adam's confession that he had heard God's voice shows that he acknowledged God's rulership and his own disobedience.

   When parents and teachers present God and His Word to children, and as the children learn to acknowledge their guilt and repentance, they will develop a keen ear for God's voice.

   The law of God, as passed on by parents to children, *must not be presented as the law of the parents.* Parents must diligently teach the law of God, with open Bible in hand and build children's obedience to the God of their parents (Deuteronomy 6:1-9). If this is done faithfully, the children will continue to hear and discern the voice of God, long after they have outgrown the necessity for close parental instruction.

3. **Teach your children "to discern [to distinguish between] both good and evil" (Hebrews 5:14).**

   Our physical senses may be trained to increase their awareness of our physical environment, and to react when they sense danger or specific stimuli, such as food, delicate weather shifts, and significant changes.

   In the same way, we are to train our children's spiritual senses and awareness. With proper training and encouragement, a child can develop an acute ability to discriminate between the godly and the ungodly, and to wisely choose the good and profitable (II Timothy 3:15-17). A bank teller who has been trained by touching only genuine dollar notes will immediately and accurately discern and discriminate counterfeit notes!

4. **Teach your children to take dominion over and subdue the earth (Genesis 1:28).**

By divine mandate, God gave man the power and the command to take dominion or rule over all lesser created things and to protect that dominion from enemies.

To exercise dominion, man must have a revelation of his purpose and potential, and release that potential to accomplish God's purposes in the earth. Unfortunately, man hasn't always been willing to obediently fulfill his responsibilities.

As Christian parents practice dominion and rulership, and walk in authority and responsible rulership as God demands, their children will learn from them and share the responsibilities and blessings of the covenant. (See Deuteronomy 28:1-14.)

While the ability to exercise dominion is inherent within the potential of each child, *it must be developed*. This is done by:

a. giving our children a knowledge of God's works and His principles of success,
b. teaching them to earn the right to rule through hard work, and,
c. blessing our children and grandchildren, thus calling forth the potential already placed within them by God, the Creator.

5. **Teach your children the value of work.**

We need to teach our children the value of work, not only in relationship to character development and discipline, but in its direct link to ownership, rulership and the exercise of authority.

They are furthermore to view work not as a curse, but as a blessing designed by God to produce fulfillment, self-worth, and godly character.

6. **Teach your children to have truth in the inward parts (Psalm 51:6).**

The Psalmist David committed adultery and murder and attempted to cover up his sin. However, at the point of repentance, confession and seeking restoration by God, David names as a condition for his re-instatement with God, the importance of truth "in the inward parts." To accomplish this, parents are to carefully monitor a child's responses, attitudes and words, and to always see to what extent they measure up to TRUTH. Always insist on honesty, self-examination, and confession of what is true.

7. **Teach your children the absolutes of God's Word.**

If we truly love our children, we will teach them the necessity for upholding and living within the limits of truth. With a knowledge of Jesus, the Truth, comes a fear of the Lord and an awareness of the snares of untruth. The wrongs of a world without absolutes can only be corrected by leaders firmly grounded in THE ABSOLUTE, Jesus Christ.

Who Will Teach Our Children?

Are we going to let our children be educated by the world and the ungodly teachers who often dominate the public schools? Or will they be educated under the influence of God's Word?

One of my sons had a teacher in a public school who worshipped the devil. Another had a teacher who seemed afraid of his own shadow. He was a frightened and emotional wreck. We were directed to start a Christian school because of such challenges as these.

In our Christian school, we know exactly what our children are being taught, and we do not hire non-Christian teachers. As a parent, I closely follow my children's total education program. I allow no one to "offend" them by the use of secular and humanistic curricula. Why? The Word of God says:

> But whoso shall offend one of these little ones which believe in me, it were better for him that a millstone were hanged about his neck, and that he were drowned in the depth of the sea.
>
> Matthew 18:6

Recently, we employed a new male teacher, and before school even started, I advised him, "Be very discreet in your actions, particularly around the girls." I did that because there have been several incidents in which female students have been harassed by male teachers in our public schools.

We need to know who is teaching our children, and ensure that they exemplify the highest Christian conduct before their students in word and deed.

Public Or Christian Schools?

Should we send our children to public or to Christian schools? I've heard many parents from North America and Europe tell me, "Let the children decide when they get older where they want to go to school." But that is wrong! As parents, it is up to us to decide where our children will be educated. If our children were mature and informed enough to make such a decision, then they certainly wouldn't need to be attending primary or secondary schools!

I strongly advocate Christian schools, with Bible-based curricula, an emphasis on academic excellence, and a total whole-man concept of education and development.

The question should not be, "Can we afford it?" but rather, "Can we afford NOT to have our children taught in Christian schools?"

Some Christian families may have to put their children's tuition at a higher priority than a second car or installment payments on luxury items. Let us carefully reconsider the actual cost to us, our children and the next generation if we do *not* invest in good Christian education for our seed.

It is thrilling to see children who have hidden the Word of God in their hearts because of the teaching of godly parents and teachers. We must teach our children to memorize and confess God's Word. Christian schools have reported general all-around improvement in memory of students where Bible passages or verses are memorized regularly!

The program of every Christian school should include memorization of scripture passages. The Book of Proverbs, the Psalms, the gospels and the epistles contain excellent material. Teach God's Word faithfully and watch your children's growth in knowledge, understanding and wisdom!

What is God asking of us as parents, and especially of women? Joel 2:28 holds a promise for our children.

> **And it shall come to pass afterward, that I will pour out my spirit upon all flesh; and your sons and your daughters shall prophesy....**

Our sons and daughters *shall* prophesy. Our righteous seed *shall* prophesy! We read of an opposite situation, however, in Amos 2:10-12, where God said:

> **Also I brought you up from the land of Egypt, and led you forty years through the wilderness, to possess the land of the Amorite.**
>
> **And I raised up of your sons for prophets, and of your young men for Nazarites. Is it not even thus, O ye children of Israel? saith the Lord.**
>
> **But ye gave the Nazarites wine to drink; and commanded the prophets, saying, Prophesy not.**

This is a message to mothers. Just as it is important to give our children nutritious meals in the natural, so in the spiritual we must obey what God commands when bringing up our righteous seed! It is shocking to believe that a godly Jewish parent would give wine to a child, chosen by God to be a Nazarite.

We break a pledge just as solemn, and show just as much disobedience and rebellion when we do not bring up our children in the nurture and admonition of the Lord, and when we fail to feed them the right spiritual food.

Mothers who live lascivious, promiscuous lives in front of their teenage daughters are giving their daughters polluted wine to drink. A Nazarite vow signified separation from the flesh, and purity of living in the Spirit.

Samson was a Nazarite, called from his mother's womb to deliver God's people from the Philistines. Samson's mother was barren, but an angel of the Lord came to her with a promise of seed:

> Now therefore beware, I pray thee, and drink not wine nor strong drink, and eat not any unclean thing:
>
> For, lo, thou shalt conceive, and bear a son; and no razor shall come on his head: for the child shall be a Nazarite unto God from the womb: *and he shall begin to deliver Israel out of the hand of the Philistines*.
>
> **Judges 13:4,5**

The angel repeated the message to the child's father in Verse 14. As spiritual head of the home with the ultimate responsibility for his family's spiritual welfare, this father had to be aware of and facilitate the fulfillment of God's requirements for his son as well as for his wife:

> *She* may not eat of any thing that cometh of the vine, neither let *her* drink wine or strong drink, nor eat any unclean thing: all that I have commanded *her* let *her* observe.
>
> **Judges 13:14**

God gave the parents of Samson some very specific commands concerning the birth and parenting of their young "nation deliverer"!

Do you want your children to be deliverers of your nation? Then God will make some demands of *you!* He demands righteous living of us. Unrighteous flirting, lascivious and promiscuous living are not God's plan for us, women. What we say to men, how we flutter our eyes, and how we hug them must be godly or else eliminated.

God was very demanding of the parents of Nazarites, and He is even more demanding with the parents of His divinely-appointed Nation Builders in Christ.

He commands in His Word that we be good teachers and godly examples to our children. Let us set and personally uphold godly standards as a sign of our partnership with God in the preserving of righteous seed.

As fathers and family heads work hand-in-hand with their spouses to assume the authority and responsibility they have been given by God Himself, the strength of the enemy's attack is weakened and pushed back from the territory of the home, and the future of our nations will look brighter with each new day!

6
Keep Ungodly Influences Away From Your Children!

That our sons may be as plants grown up in their youth; that our daughters may be as corner stones, polished after the similitude of a palace.

Psalm 144:12

Children absorb information and influences from their environment. In the electronic, information-rich 90's, more than ever we should be discriminating in what our children learn, and where they learn it.

A father's solemn warning is found in Proverbs 19:27, "Cease, my son, to hear the instruction that causeth to err from the words of knowledge." In other words, "Cease, My son, to listen to the instruction that is causing you to make a mistake." A young child, however, may lack that discriminating ability.

It is up to you. You must decide, as far as it is in your power, what you want your child to hear, to see and to experience.

Watch what your children view on television. Most "children's" cartoons today feature ghosts, sorcery, witchcraft, violence, or obscenity in some form or another.

I'm saddened to tell you that I still hear parents say things like, "I left my child at home. She's okay. She'll watch TV until she falls asleep." The television has become a babysitter!

51

How can we be so irresponsible! Dear parent, if you are doing this, you are not sufficiently discriminating of what your child learns.

You can teach them all you want when you are there with them, but if you put the TV in front of them to make it easier for you, you will undo all the good you have done.

The professional communicators in the electronic media specially gear their programming to capture and hold attention.

Satan skillfully uses the secular media in his diabolical plan to catch your seed and involve them in things outside God's kingdom. He uses the mesmerizing power of television and other media to TEACH your children a perspective and attitude about life that is different from the pure perspective of the Word.

When children watch gory, horrific scenes on TV, they lose their inner knowledge that the weird, the monstrous, or the evil are inherently wrong. When we let our children feast on godless television offerings (as the Israelites fed their children from the offerings to idols), our children will develop a taste for this new "food." They will lose that ability to discern the distasteful, the ugly, the disharmonic, and the obscene along with the desire to avoid them.

An early result of this ungodly diet of entertainment is that our children will want to experience everything in a heightened sort of way. You won't be able to offer them anything that is bland anymore. The music must be loud. Everything must be experienced in an extreme way, because this is what the media has fed into their lives.

We are reaping in our nations today what we have sown in the days gone by — violence, lewdness, drug abuse, pornography, profanity and vulgarity.

Jeremiah 10:2 warns us, "Thus saith the Lord, Learn not the way of the heathen...." We must not let ungodly teaching mold the minds of our seed. Our children are too impressionable, too vulnerable, and too precious for us to subject them to the influence of the world's humanistic and ruthless media.

An eight-year-old student from a public school my children once attended was asked to give her definition of "privacy" during a children's television program. She shocked the listening parents by proudly reciting, "Privacy is not letting my mother see the letter I wrote."

Our children are learning the way of the heathen secular humanists! This impressionable eight year old and thousands just like her are being subtly and carefully schooled in humanist doctrines.

These doctrines include teaching the secondary place of parental guidance and rules, the right to oppose adult scrutiny of behavior, and twisted self-centered conceptions of "equal rights" (children may decide their destinies and path just as freely as adults — or parents), and the supremacy of individual choice and decision-making.

I have found that ungodly teachers are themselves unable to guide our children. Or they reject the opportunities to guide them by offering them a "choice" at crucial times in their academic, moral, or vocational development.

Colossians 2:8 speaks directly to this type of subtle teaching which can steal the minds and hearts of an entire generation:

> **Beware lest any man spoil** (the next generation) **you through philosophy and vain deceit, after the tradition of men, after the rudiments** (principles) **of this world, and not after Christ.**

The word "spoil" may be translated, "to steal away the best that you have." Vain philosophies and humanistic ideologies will captivate and destroy the best that we have — our children!

The first Psalm offers concerned parents some good advice about controlling what their seed listens to, the company they keep, whose advice they seek and how they spend their leisure time.

> **Blessed is the man that walketh not in the counsel of the ungodly, nor standeth in the way of sinners, nor sitteth in the seat of the scornful.**
>
> **But his delight is in the law of the Lord; and in his law doth he meditate day and night.**
>
> **Psalm 1:1,2**

These scriptures provide a sweeping summary of negative, self-indulgent activities, as opposed to meditation, delight, and total absorption in that which pleases God.

Romans 16:19 says, "...I would have you wise unto that which is good, and simple concerning evil." The word 'simple' in this verse means "ignorant of, inexperienced in, or unsullied by" that which is evil. It is a naive parent who believes the myth that a child needs to be exposed to evil in order to choose the good!

Our constant prayer as parents must be, "Father, help us to be wise in the formal and informal education of our righteous seed. Help us to carefully guard our children's minds and to screen out, whenever possible, these influences which do not give life to our children."

When Should We Begin To Teach Our Seed?

Isaiah the prophet rebuked "the drunkards of Ephraim" who led the nation of Israel. Noting that their love for strong drink caused them to err in their vision and stumble in judgment, he mentions the necessity to teach God's Word patiently and simply to the very young.

> **Whom shall he teach knowledge? and whom shall he make to understand doctrine? them that are weaned from the milk and drawn from the breasts.**

**For precept must be (taught) upon precept, precept
upon precept; line upon line, line upon line; here a
little, and there a little.**

                                        Isaiah 28:9,10

Wise and righteous leaders can only be raised up
through this type of thorough grounding in God's
unchanging Word.

We are not to neglect to teach our children. Those
seemingly endless repetitions of elementary lessons lay the
foundation for sound doctrine and the fear of the Lord that
is so necessary for successful living. These things combine
to help form a spirit in our children that is naturally turned
towards spiritual things. These provide for a holy lifestyle
and a rich spiritual inheritance.

Some time ago while in Europe, I attended a baptism
service conducted by a friend for the nineteen-year-old son
of a minister. I had to wonder, "Why had he waited so
long?"

I learned that the boy's parents, although they were
ministers of the Gospel, had not introduced their son to the
scriptural truths about water baptism until his teens because
they felt that "this decision-making activity should be
postponed until the child was much older."

He was now nineteen. His parents and teachers waited
until their child had reached a "certain level of maturity"
to introduce some truths requiring individual decision-
making. "In his own time he would make his own
decisions," I was told.

This sort of reasoning sounds very noble and
sophisticated, but it is contrary to God's Word and to
common experience as well.

The spirit of a very young child is naturally open to
spiritual truths which are conveyed spiritually, and his or
her ability to grasp the things of God has little to do with

stages of intellectual development or with the acquisition of social maturity.

Listen, Christian parent: the enemy wants to steal your righteous seed. Satan will do all in his power to steal that soul long before he is eighteen or nineteen — the time when we are expecting him to have come to some developmental "age of accountability." The enemy has no problem advancing his particular world views or 'religious' views to our children.

It's time for us to stop apologizing for our beliefs and faith in Christ. Either we are right or we are not. It is time for us to take a stand and raise our children accordingly, without apology. We need to be alert to the tricks of the enemy.

The Word of God is straightforward, and totally clear: "Train up a child in the way he should go; and when he is old, he will not depart from it" (Proverbs 22:6).

To *train* in Hebrew means "to touch the palate." This word may also be used to describe the technique used by mothers to train their infants to appreciate and swallow solid food.

It is a fact: whatever food a baby is given first in a particular culture (be it Italian or Mexican), that will be a favorite choice above other foods introduced later.

The same is true in the Spirit realm. Give your young child a diet of spiritual milk in infancy and ensure a lifelong preference for spiritual food!

God spoke in detail about child-rearing through the Psalmist in Psalm 92:13-15:

> **Those that be planted in the house of the Lord shall flourish in the courts of our God.**
>
> **They shall still bring forth fruit in old age; they shall be fat and flourishing;**

**To shew that the Lord is upright: he is my rock,
and there is no unrighteousness in him.**

This means that we are to plant our children in the
Word of God. The problem with many children is that they
are not rooted or planted anywhere. Children who are
planted in the house of the Lord will flourish in the courts
of God. As we "plant" our children in the church, or in
a Christian school, or in a Biblically-sound education
program, they will flourish in our nations. When they are
old, they will still show forth fruit — the fruit of the Spirit!

I urge you to "plant" your children in the house of the
Lord and in the Word of God. If you do this, your children
will literally *show that the Lord is upright* (Verse 15). God is
looking for living testimonials of His glory and faithfulness.

When our children are planted and rooted in God, they
become literal, living testimonies of His faithfulness in a
faithless world. Their lifestyles will reflect a prosperity and
favor that is both supernatural and natural. Proverbs 24:4
promotes acquiring godly knowledge and wisdom with an
outstanding promise of reward: "And by knowledge shall
the chambers be filled with all precious and pleasant riches."

Some of us are so selfish. We fix our attention and
affections on our efforts to preserve ourselves and our own
seed, and think little about being a testimony to God. I pray
that our sons and daughters will rise up to be a testimony
— not to any particular ministry or household — but to
God's faithfulness!

God is vitally interested, for His own sake, in raising
up living monuments in this godless world — monuments
to His supernatural ability and desire as a Heavenly Father
to provide for His children. And His will should be our own
desire as well.

7

Absolutes: God's Anchor
For An Unstable Generation

> For I will pour water upon him that is thirsty, and
> floods upon the dry ground: I will pour my spirit upon
> thy seed, and my blessing upon thine offspring:
>
> And they shall spring up as among the grass, as
> willows by the water courses.
>
> One shall say, I am the Lord's; and another shall
> call himself by the name of Jacob; and another shall
> subscribe with his hand unto the Lord, and surname
> himself by the name of Israel.
>
> Isaiah 44:3-5

God expects Christian parents to actively participate
in the education of their righteous seed. Whether we become
involved in their education or not, our children will be
influenced and instructed by some set of standards — either
ours or someone else's.

Children need to learn standards based on absolutes.
The Christian life is based on the truth that right is right
and wrong is wrong. Jesus said, "...I am the way, the
truth, and the life..." (John 14:6). We should teach our
children that all truth is rooted in Christ Jesus, and we
should teach this without apology or excuse.

All too often, men and women pay other people to
teach their children while they pursue a job or a career.
Unfortunately, these individuals (or institutions!) often
destroy our seed by teaching them that right is no longer

right, or that a "right" choice "depends upon the circumstances."

Our children may learn to say, "I can do this, because I feel like doing it," or "I can do it, because in this circumstance, it is all right," or "My parents are doing it."

We must teach absolutes. Truth is never dependent on circumstances. Behavior should not be dictated by feelings or moods. If your child's feelings or moods determine behavior, you may certainly expect trouble in the future. As parents, we should never send conflicting messages to our children by living carelessly ourselves and making decisions based only on what seems convenient or self-gratifying.

We are to teach our children the fear of the Lord, which is "...the beginning of wisdom: and the knowledge of the holy is understanding" (Proverbs 9:10). If we are not careful, our children will be more afraid of man and of what their peers say, than they are of God and of what His Word says.

All of our standards must be based upon the Word of God. When we train and correct our children, we should not say, "I am going to spank you now because you disobeyed me. I have told you time and time again, 'Do not do so-and-so.' "

Instead, open God's Word and say, "God's Word says...." Base every rule that you make upon the Word of God. Then say, "God has given me authority and responsibility for you." Establish that authority when they are young, because in the public schools, your young child is being taught that he has "privacy"! His right to "privacy" is equal or superior to your rights as a parent he is told. Some teachers are even saying that you have no right, mother, even to look at the letter of your eight year old! This is humanist and wrong.

When you face conflict with a child's defiant disobedience and self-will, stand on your delegated authority and say, "God has given me this authority." Mother, hold on to the authority given by God, and to the authority given by the head of your household, your husband. Say, "Son, I am going to punish you because so-and-so has happened. God's Word says...."

Always make and support your disciplinary stand and parental decisions with the Word of God!

Why Should We Bring The Bible Into Parenting?

It is important to base your actions, reactions, decisions and discipline upon God's Word, *because His Word never changes*. This is true for individuals, parents, lawmakers and national leaders. It is the surest way to set godly standards for our children.

If you justify your rules or decisions with phrases such as, "This is what my great-grandmother always said," or, "My mother always used to do it this way, so this is how we will do it in this house," then you need to find the real root behind those rules and decisions. When you make your decisions and set guidelines based on God's Word, then you can honestly and authoritatively state: "It's God's way."

Many of us approach the supernatural tasks of parenting in our own strength and personal authority. We need to go back to the source of all power: the Word of God and God Himself. The book of Proverbs sums it up: "Every wise woman buildeth her house..." (14:1); and, "Through wisdom is a house builded; and by understanding it is established" (24:3).

The only sure way to build a child's life and educate him or her is to build that precious "house" upon the sure foundation of knowledge and wisdom in God's Word. This alone will equip that child with the wisdom to make good decisions for life today and eternity tomorrow.

Our Children Imitate Us

When an unwanted phone call comes, or an unwelcome guest knocks on your door, do you tell your child, "Just say that I am busy or that I am sleeping" — when you are neither busy nor asleep? You may think lightly of it, but your child will be confused about what truth is.

Whenever an important person teaches a child to lie, that child will think that it is all right to tell a lie, and will become confused about truth. Isaiah 38:19 says, "...the father to the children shall make known thy truth."

When parents' daily actions are determined by selfish or carnal motives or are dependent on mere moods, feelings or convenience, then children will also learn to live that way. Children live what they learn.

Separate Right From Wrong

Teach your children the difference between right and wrong, between "the holy and the profane." The Bible records what happened to two children of a priest named Aaron in the book of Leviticus. We sometimes say, "But that is the Old Testament, the days under the law. God *used* to be like that." God's ways have never changed.

God carefully taught Aaron how to offer the sacrifices in the temple. His instructions were careful, detailed, and meticulous regarding the priestly duties and spiritual observances. Despite Aaron's detailed training, he failed to pass down his respect for the things of God to his sons. Their outright disobedience triggered God's quick, just and fatal response.

> **And Nadab and Abihu, the sons of Aaron, took either of them his censer, and put fire therein, and put incense thereon, and offered strange fire before the Lord, which he commanded them not.**
>
> **And there went out fire from the Lord, and devoured them, and they died before the Lord.**

> Then Moses said unto Aaron, This is it that the
> Lord spake, saying, I will be sanctified in them that
> come nigh me, and before all the people I will be
> glorified. And Aaron held his peace.
>
> Leviticus 10:1-3

Every time I read this passage, I feel Aaron's dread of God's wrath, and a sense of sorrow for this father-priest in that tragic situation. Aaron held his peace because he could offer no acceptable answer. Either he taught his sons wrongly, he did not teach them enough, they were forgetful hearers, or they did not take God seriously.

What about you and me? Will we stand helplessly by and watch our children reap the consequences of their disobedience? (Or is it our disobedience?)

Modern Christian parents often suffer from a "theological" problem. They believe that God is a merciful God, but they forget about His other equally important attributes. God is indeed merciful. The Bible says His mercies are new every morning, but it also tells us He is a *holy* and *just* God! He has placed eternal laws in motion that affect our lives. One of them establishes that we reap what we sow. When we disobey God's laws and commandments, we reap His correction and punishments.

I have a word of warning for mothers and fathers: if your child does something wrong today, forgive him before the day is over. Get up tomorrow, and do not say anything about that wrong again. Your mercy, too, must be "new every morning." Your child must know that the slate is clean. If you continue to rehearse that problem and "hit" your child with it time and time again, he or she will not understand the mercy of God.

In Leviticus 10:10, after listing a number of guidelines and regulations for godly living, God explained that He gave His law, ". . . that ye may put difference between holy and unholy and between unclean and clean."

There are absolute, distinct differences between holy and unholy, clean and unclean. There are no blurred or gray areas where individual choice may be exercised to commit wrong under the guise of ignorance. This type of "situational justification" can undermine the character of the justice and holiness of God.

One verse later in Leviticus 10:11, God says, "And that ye may teach the children of Israel all the statutes which the Lord hath spoken unto them by the hand of Moses." God wants to restore His standards in the church and in our nations. For our part, we are to teach our children the difference between good and evil.

Teach God's Word Diligently

Since God blesses nations through their children, the righteous seed, the importance of those children can't be overstated. The enemy is out to destroy our seed, because he knows that out of the mouths of babes and sucklings, strength has been ordained (Psalm 8:2).

Don't be deceived. The devil wants to pluck from our children's hearts everything that we have taught them. We must teach them well enough to resist the devil on their own when we are not around. Thirty-minute Sunday school teachings every week will not get the job done. God requires much more than that.

God's principles must completely infiltrate the very fabric of life of the next generation. If we build the Word into our national life, we will change the entire culture. This can happen only when Biblical standards infiltrate our educational systems, literature, the arts, the civic systems and every other aspect of national life. Then we will begin to see righteousness established in our nation.

First of all, we cannot teach something that we do not practice ourselves. That kind of schizophrenic living will confuse and disillusion our children. We must keep the commandments ourselves.

God commanded Moses and the children of Israel:

> Now these are the commandments, the statutes, and the judgments, which the Lord your God commanded to teach you, that ye might do them in the land whither ye go to possess it:
>
> That thou mightest fear the Lord thy God, to keep all his statutes and his commandments, which I command thee, *thou, and thy son, and thy son's sons,* all the days of thy life; and that thy days may be prolonged.
>
> Deuteronomy 6:1,2

How much effort do we exert to ensure the spiritual development of our children? Many times we overfeed ourselves while our children remain spiritually underweight and malnourished. We may attend or even host numerous adult conferences every year, but what about our children? Our children are waiting to learn.

Jehovah God gives parents a direct command in a pivotal passage found in Deuteronomy 6:6-9:

> And these words, which I command thee this day, shall be in thine heart:
>
> And thou shalt teach them *diligently* unto thy children, and shalt talk of them when thou sittest in thine house, and when thou walkest by the way, and when thou liest down, and when thou risest up.
>
> And thou shalt bind them for a sign upon thine hand, and they shall be as frontlets between thine eyes.
>
> And thou shalt write them upon the posts of thy house, and on thy gates.

The sixth chapter of Deuteronomy also outlines three benefits or "side effects" promised to those who fear God and keep His commandments:

1. Our days will be prolonged (Verse 2).

2. There will be national health and well-being (Verse 3).

3. The righteous seed of a godly nation will "increase mightily" (Verse 3).

We must speak to our children about God's Word, His commandments and His statutes, as we walk by the way, as we lie down and as we rise up. We should be totally absorbed in the purposeful activity of teaching God's ways to our children.

There is more! In Deuteronomy 6:20,21, parents are exhorted:

> **And when thy son asketh thee in time to come, saying, What mean the testimonies, and the statutes, and the judgments, which the Lord our God hath commanded you?**
>
> **Then thou shalt say unto thy son, We were Pharaoh's bondmen in Egypt; and the Lord brought us out of Egypt with a mighty hand.**

When your children ask, "Mommy, Daddy, why do we have to do such-and-such?" take the time to explain the Biblical roots of your daily walk with God. Say, "Son, here is where we are coming from. Daughter, this is the way God has provided for us, and this is why we are doing this."

Take the time to explain God's ways to your children. If necessary, go back in the history of your people. "God preserved and brought your great-great-grandparents to this country. They were a strong and fearless people...."

In all things, acknowledge the Lord in your own history and tell your children about God's hand, His providence, and His dealings with your family, your ancestors, your race and your nation.

Sometimes we have poor memories of God's blessings. God wants us to remember and to pass those memories on to our righteous seed. Then God's blessings for our people

— the blessings of wealth, long life, well-being and peace
— will be ours to inherit and to pass on to our seed.

8

Battle Strategies
For Determined Parents

For God will save Zion, and will build the cities
of Judah: that they may dwell there, and have it in
possession.

The seed also of his servants shall inherit it: and
they that love his name shall dwell therein.
                                                    Psalm 69:35,36

God gave me a vision that inspired this book and its
urgent message. I live with the burden of the vision day
and night. It's a recurring panoramic vision of profane
articulators of godless philosophies, silenced church leaders,
helpless and bereft mothers and abused children.

It is indeed the vision which Jesus sees always and
which He urges us to see and respond to. With spiritual
eyes and the heart of Jesus, let us see and feel the darkness
of our city, the sadness and fear of its children, the
ruthfulness of its exploiters and the utter helplessness of
its leaders. We have a global problem. God calls it sin; man
calls it everything but sin.

I believe in a loving God with all my heart. Yet I also
believe the words of Jesus in Matthew 5:13, where He
described the people of God as "the salt of the world." He
urged us to be salty, or be cast aside by the world as
worthless. God's people literally act as a preservative
wherever they are found — in government, in the churches,
in communities and school boards, and in civic groups.

Without our strong, vibrant influence and corrective force for good, our societies are destined to decay.

As Christian parents, we can no longer distance ourselves from the struggles of our nation and society. The things we do or do not do today will affect the lives and destinies of our children tomorrow!

After I saw and experienced the pain of the natural calamities that struck my island nation of Jamaica, I sought the face of God. I wanted answers.

Through His Word, and with dreams and visions, God impressed upon my spirit the great urgency we face if our children are to survive. We must take a bold and determined stand as Christian parents to raise up nation builders for the next generation!

May God's Spirit quicken you so that you will not distance yourself from your people — from your own flesh and blood, and yes, from the children of your nation.

Who Or What Is The Enemy?

What are we to do about the situations we face? What threatens our homes and children, and triggers the impending judgment of a holy God on an unrighteous generation?

One of the most deadly and prevalent threats is the godless, humanistic ideology that has engulfed our schools, governments and media. The nations are dying and decaying from within. Our sons and daughters are being engulfed by the persuasive voices teaching godless ideologies in the public schools, awash in hopelessness and despair. What can we do about it?

It is time to go to war! God Himself established eternal enmity between the first woman, Eve, and Satan; and between her Seed, Jesus Christ the Messiah, and Satan. God has ordained that with this supernatural enmity would come a supernatural boldness and power for parents throughout the generations to preserve the seed — the seed which held the promise of salvation through Christ. (See Romans 16:20; Galatians 3:16; and Colossians 2:15.)

The *Law of Equivalent Effect* in Genesis 3:15 clearly establishes that the God-given enmity established in the garden long ago still exists, and that it is accompanied by a supernaturally endowed power for the preservation of our children.

The Hope Of Our Nations

In a way, even as mankind's hope rested on the arrival of the Divine Seed who became the Messiah, so the hope of our nations and churches today rests on the arrival and timely maturation of our precious seed.

Satan has always directed his anger and evil plots towards the seed, and he still targets the seed of godly parents — but we don't have to stand for it!

Women, we must develop a strategy. Strategy stirs and intrigues us. Consider Moses' mother. She had to devise a strategy to save her seed. This determined mother from the priestly tribe of Levi risked her life to save her son.

She defied the decree of Pharaoh and hid Moses for three months. When she could no longer conceal her son safely, she made an ark of bulrushes and carefully waterproofed it with pitch. Then she placed the ark in some overgrowth near the spot where the daughter of Pharaoh bathed each day, and her daughter watched from a hidden place nearby.

Her heroic defiance of Pharaoh, along with some skillful planning, saved the life of her newborn son and preserved the line of the Messiah. It's amusing to see how God turned the situation around so that Pharaoh's daughter brought up Moses, and Pharaoh unknowingly paid Moses' mother for the upbringing of the very child who would later defeat him and deliver Israel out of his hands!

This act by Moses' mother crushed Satan's plan to destroy Abraham's seed, and it paved the way for the freedom of an entire nation in direct fulfillment of God's prophetic word concerning the Seed of the Woman.

Pharaoh's wanton destruction of the male children as recorded in Exodus 1:16-22 was yet another of Satan's unsuccessful attempts to destroy and annihilate the seed of the woman.

In Exodus 4, God spoke to Moses concerning His unyielding desire to save Israel:

> **And thou shalt say unto Pharaoh, Thus saith the Lord, Israel is my son, even my firstborn;**
>
> **And I say unto thee, Let my son go, that he may serve me: and if thou refuse to let him go, behold, I will slay thy son, even thy firstborn.**
>
> **Exodus 4:22,23**

Most of us are familiar with Pharaoh's stubborn rebellion and with Moses' pleas to him to let God's people go. Pharaoh's heart remained hardened in spite of the terrible plagues God promised and delivered.

Then God struck His most powerful blow: He struck down Pharaoh's seed because he refused to release God's seed — Israel. It should be clear to any serious student of the Bible: the real battle in Exodus 4 was not for manpower or for land. It was a battle for the SEED.

This episode also shows us that God thinks of nations in terms of sons. "...Israel is my son...my firstborn..." (Exodus 4:22). God said in Verse 23, "If you do not let My son go, I am going to kill your son." God meant business when He said that.

When He saw Pharaoh's obstinate determination to hold captive the children of God, God had to send the death angel and all of Egypt's firstborn sons were slain. Only then did Pharaoh let the sons of God go free.

Parents, there is a battle going on in the heavenlies over the nations of the earth, and there are also continuous "ground attacks." We are fighting for our sons and daughters.

Many of us may understand that the weapons of our warfare are not carnal but spiritual, but how many of us are prepared to be just as determined and relentless as God is in the preservation of our children from the deadly darts of Satan? Look at the determination of God to free His children from Pharaoh. Are we as determined in our personal battle for our seed?

Daily skirmishes come, but at times we may find ourselves in a "head-on" major clash with the enemy or with death itself. Are we prepared and ready?

My Personal Battle

Only a few years ago, a critical event in my own life changed my entire approach to warfare for the righteous seed. My husband was off to a camp outing. Have you noticed, women, that very often when the husband and father is away, the enemy will try to raise havoc with family members? He tried it at our house, but his calculated shot did not succeed.

The devil chose the time when my husband was away for his diabolical attempt to take the life of my fourteen-year-old son. Young Carrington Peter first complained of a sudden, severe pain in the late evening. By 10:00 o'clock that night, he said, "Mummy, I feel so badly." I comforted him as much as I could, and tried to ignore the fears I felt about the serious sound of his complaint. Again he said, "Mummy, I have a real bad pain. I need to go to the doctor." By midnight, the pain was unbearable.

When my husband arrived home a short time later, I met him at the driveway and shouted, "Don't park the car. You must take Peter to the doctor immediately!"

By 10:00 the next morning, Peter received emergency surgery after the doctors diagnosed acute appendicitis. The Holy Spirit guided the doctor to the root of the pain, even though the devil tried to camouflage the source of the problem!! The veteran anesthetist who attended the surgery later said, "That was the nastiest appendix I have ever seen."

Apparently, the venom from the ruptured appendix had spread itself into the surrounding tissues so quickly that Peter would have been dead if we had waited. This plot was the enemy's attempt to destroy righteous seed.

I'll never forget that night. As I waited to hear news from the hospital, plaintive funeral songs floated into my mind, planted there by the destroyer. The enemy was telling me that I might as well get ready for a funeral!

These dark thoughts kept intruding into my mind and spirit, trying to sap my strength, my hope and my faith. Suddenly, I became totally alert to the devil's subversive devices!! Even though I was tired and sleepy, a supernatural and renewed strength flowed into me. I jumped up and cursed death! I walked the floor, and again and again I declared aloud, "I curse death in the name of Jesus, and I fight for the life of my child." I waged spiritual warfare until a note of victory was won in my spirit.

I thank God today that He helped me exercise God-given dominion and authority over death and speak the law of Life on behalf of my righteous seed. God has given to us this tool of dominion (Romans 8:2).

The battle is on for our seed, but God is saying to the enemy, "Set my children free." In other words, God was, and still is, prepared to deliver our children whom we have sanctified and set apart for His purposes.

In another and wider sense, sons and daughters across our nation are being destroyed by drugs, disease, accidents, crime and suicide. These children need the intercession and the war cry of mothers who will do battle on their behalf with the enemy. Satan has a masterful plot designed to destroy our seed and weaken our nation. We must offensively confront these abuses with spiritual as well as physical tools.

God's Midwives Stood In The Gap For The Seed

When cruel affliction, hard bondage, and grueling slavery failed to exterminate the Israelites, Pharaoh devised yet another plan to destroy the male children of Israel. I believe the devil planted this scheme in Pharaoh's mind so that the promised Seed, the Messiah, would not come. (See Genesis 3:15 and Romans 16:20.)

Pharaoh told the Hebrew midwives, ''...When ye do the office of a midwife to the Hebrew women, and see them upon the stools; if it be a son, then ye shall kill him: but if it be a daughter, then she shall live.'' (Exodus 1:16).

God's divine plan was not to be thwarted. He had prepared the midwives. Exodus 1:17 declares, ''But the midwives feared God and did not as the king of Egypt commanded them, but saved the men children alive.'' Glory to God!!

My plea to mothers, to fathers, and to grandparents is, ''Be midwives and save the children alive.'' How do we do that? By interceding on behalf of our nation. By intercepting, through spiritual warfare, the blows of the destroyer (Satan). By fearlessly protecting our children from the devil's plots to pollute, control, and finally exterminate God's heritage, our children.

God rewarded the faithful midwives in Exodus 1:20,21:

Therefore God dealt well with the midwives: and the people multiplied, and waxed very mighty.

> **And it came to pass, because the midwives feared God, that He made them houses.**

When the Word says God made them "houses," it does not mean He gave them pretty buildings on a hill. The word translated "houses" refers to generations. It means that God gave them rulership. Generations and rulership. That is God's promise to us today. Our children are being targeted for destruction by a vengeful and vindictive enemy.

We must preserve the life of our seed by our swift, wise and skillful spiritual midwifery. We must boldly refuse to obey the dictates of any cruel system which Satan uses to kill our seed. Then the blessings will come as our children rise up and are prepared for the deliverance of and leadership in our nations.

Preserve the Seed Through Faith and Action

Woven into the history of the Hebrews is the poignant account of the Shunammite woman who fought for the life of her son (II Kings 4). Her outstanding hospitality to Elisha the prophet, and her persistent good works in the face of nearly hopeless circumstances won her the promise and gift of a son.

This woman was created by God to be a life-giver, and thus she was empowered with supernatural faith to believe God for new life for her child. The life-force within her activated her, in the face of seemingly impossible odds, to have victory over death in any form.

This mother's relentless struggle of faith for the resurrection of her dead child typifies the kind of battle which every woman of God should be prepared to wage.

What were the weapons of her warfare? First, she was completely immersed in her determination that life would be restored. Second, she was unwilling to choose the path of mourning. And thirdly, she refused to give in to the negative circumstances confronting her. Indeed, this mother devoted her energy and faith to the selfless pursuit of life for her child.

Her faith was sustained until Elisha said, "Call this Shunammite" and "Take up thy son." This mother's quick and decisive actions helped release God's miraculous power to *restore her seed to life!*

This is the path to victory, the strategy which places our feet squarely on the serpent's head for a crushing victory. The Shunammite woman trusted in a living God who not only endows with life but also sustains life. She discovered that God collaborates with His children who choose themselves to be life-givers with Him.

One of the most gripping descriptions of a mother's heart cry is found in Verse 27, "...And the man of God said, Let her alone; for her soul is vexed within her...."

Have you had to go to battle? Have you confronted Satan or a spirit of death? God sees the heart of a woman whose "soul is vexed within her." We have been formed by God to receive a seed, to carry and nurture a fetus, a living soul within our bodies, and have been given the grace to parent and nurture life.

But we have also been given the capacity to love much, to love our children more than ourselves. This turns into a driving "vexation" when our children are hurt or attacked. This vexation equips us with the supernatural fortitude and aggressiveness necessary for the protection and survival of our righteous seed.

How To Win The Fight

The Shunammite woman's earnestness in prayer and depth of sorrow also typify the tender account of Hannah, the barren wife of Elkanah, who longed for a child. Her loneliness and shame were provoked by her adversary, the jealous Peninah (the other wife), who gloated over her many children.

Hannah's anguish is expressed in I Samuel 1:10, "And she was in bitterness of soul, and prayed unto the Lord, and wept sore."

In Verse 15, she told Eli the priest, "...I am a woman of a sorrowful spirit: I have drunk neither wine nor strong drink, but have poured out my soul before the Lord."

Not many of us have experienced the depth of Hannah's sorrow and bitterness of soul. But we can all benefit from her determination to be the incubator of righteous seed and to dedicate that seed to the service of God.

Hannah's solemn promise to God was fulfilled in I Samuel 1:27,28.

> **For this child I prayed; and the Lord hath given me my petition which I asked of him;**

> **Therefore also I have lent him to the Lord; as long as he liveth he shall be lent to the Lord.**

Why does a woman seek seed? Hannah offered God the very thing she desired most. It was not merely a symbolic offer. She literally gave up Samuel to minister in the temple and be educated as a priest and judge of Israel (I Samuel 1:21).

God is still seeking parents (Elkanah also made a vow) who will raise up righteous seed to serve God as spiritual priests, leaders and judges of their nations.

The lives, struggles and victories of Moses' mother, the Shunammite woman, and Hannah reveal that *the battle for the seed* is waged before our seed is conceived, throughout the life of the seed, and then into the life of the next generation.

As Christian parents, we have the clear testimony of God's Word that we have the weapons to preserve the seed within us through the power of God!

Many generations after the miraculous birth and ministry of Moses, Mary, the mother of Jesus, had to hide and flee into Egypt to preserve her seed. The precious seed in her womb was destined to bruise the head of the enemy. (See Genesis 3:15 and Matthew 2:13-18.)

She was supernaturally warned of Satan's attempt to kill her seed. The emergency escape to Egypt delivered her son from the slaughter of thousands of infants, all within a ten-mile radius of Bethlehem.

This is one of the most dramatic examples of God's faithfulness to godly parents to warn them of danger or attack. Praise God, the earthly parents of our Savior heard the plan of God for the preservation of that Child of destiny!

Attention: Single Women!

If you are a single woman, you should not feel left out. You also have a responsibility to generate life. I have known many God-fearing single women who have fostered or adopted children. God has great promises for those children who, otherwise, would be at the mercy of the enemy in some ungodly foster or adoptive home.

As women, we are natural generators of life — life-givers — and that very potential to give life also gives us the strength and wisdom to sustain and preserve life.

Satan persistently plots to destroy every seed with the potential and promise to deliver nations. At the same time, the continuing effect of that first word spoken, that the seed of the woman would bruise the head of Satan, continues to empower every mother in her perpetual battle with Satan.

This enmity, declared by God Himself, is accompanied by the *guarantee of victory* for every parent who is willing to collaborate with God.

9
Fourteen Steps To Successful Parenting

What man is he that feareth the Lord? him shall
he teach in the way that he shall choose.

His soul shall dwell at ease; and his seed shall
inherit the earth.

Psalm 25:12,13

Abraham is known as the father of the Jewish nation.
God gave this remarkable man a promise with a
generational, as well as a historical impact.

What do we know about Abraham? We know he came
from Ur, a land immersed in moon worship. Apparently,
the knowledge of God had been nearly lost on the earth.
It was in this dim spiritual climate that God spoke to a man
whose heart was open to His touch.

If we learn the main characteristics of this patriarch,
perhaps we can begin to enjoy the same success he enjoyed.
His faith in God's promise of children produced the seeds
of an entire race of people and the Messiah!

1. *Abraham had to forge new spiritual roots.* He had to develop
a godly heritage, even though his own roots could be traced
back to pagan moon worship.

All of us need a "new root" to go to heaven — we must
accept Jesus Christ as Lord and Savior. At that point, we
are grafted into a perfect spiritual root — Jesus.

In the natural realm, some of us approach the Christian life and child-rearing from more difficult starting points. Fortunately, Jesus equalizes all things through His power.

If your father was known for his alcoholism, you do not have to inherit that vulnerability, or to pass it on to your sons or daughters.

You can break the cords of any generational curse or pattern and be free of it through Christ Jesus.

Pray this short but powerful prayer and confession to cut generational ties: "In the name of Jesus Christ, and by the power of His blood, I cut the umbilical cord that binds me or my seed to the past in the following areas ... (e.g. alcohol, gluttony, etc.)."

2. *Abraham ventured into the unknown.* (See Genesis 12:1-4.) God may be saying to you, "I want you to move to this or that country." Are you willing to leave the comfortable patterns of the past and go into the future? If you have difficulty obeying God's directional word, you may doubt your own goals for life and lack vision for the next generation.

It is interesting to note that Abraham's father, Terah (See Genesis 11:31,32), had also left Ur to go to Canaan, but he took his family only as far as Haran "and dwelt there" until he died. Terah was not given a purpose, a destiny, or a promise as his son, Abraham, was!

3. *Abraham heard the covenant promise and appropriated it for his family.* (See Genesis 12:1-4.)

4. *Abraham devised strategies for the survival of his family.* He fled to Egypt (of all places) to avoid the famine. (See Genesis 12:10.)

5. He demonstrated that he had received God's promise by faith when he offered worship to God. (See Genesis 12:8.) Abraham built an altar as a permanent testimony of his trust in and thanksgiving to God.

6. Abraham was generous toward his family members. (See his generous treatment of his nephew, Lot, in Genesis 13:1-12.) Some races and nations, most notably the Jewish people, have become prosperous because they have a strong family heritage and they keep wealth within their families. They generously invest in the next generation and so perpetuate family wealth and strength. In the Christian world, some fathers lend a deaf ear to children struggling with high-interest loans and new businesses, even though they have bulging bank accounts.

7. Abraham was willing to walk through the land. (See Genesis 13:17.) God has promised us dominion over our nation, but have we even gone as far as the next town? Has God put nationhood in your heart? Does your intercession stretch beyond "me and mine" to include your neighborhood and your nation?

8. He did not fear war. In Genesis 14:14-16, Abraham fought against hostile kings to rescue his nephew. Women want strong men who will wage spiritual warfare for the salvation of their loved ones and their nations. I encourage my sons to "fight" for what they greatly desire. I also encourage my husband to guard our family offensively as well, to protect our children from the attacks of the evil one.

9. Abraham was a generous giver and tither. (See Genesis 14:18-20.) As a result, he inherited many rich blessings and became the world's wealthiest man of his day. (Malachi 3:10,11 says Abraham's children also inherited property that was richly blessed.)

10. *He craved for seed!* After he was given the promise of seed, Abraham did not forget the promise — even when decades had passed. He earnestly sought the Lord for its fulfillment. God is looking for believers today who will gird up themselves like Job and reason with Him. (See Job 38:3; 40:7; 42:4.) In Job 38-40, God called Job to speak up, like only a father can, for renewed blessings for himself and his family. Abraham asked God a sincere question concerning the promise of seed that would be numberless as the stars: "...whereby shall I know that I shall inherit it?" (Genesis 15:8).

11. Genesis 15:11 says *Abraham drove the fowls away from his covenant sacrifice.* A covenant promise may have been given to us, but vultures will try to devour the prophetic promises given for our children. Unless we drive away these emissaries of Satan, we will have nothing to show for it.

12. *Abraham submitted himself to all the terms and requirements of the covenant.* (See Genesis 15:12.) God may require something painful of us, but we must submit ourselves to it if we are to reap the reward.

13. *Abraham was willing to have a name change.* (See Genesis 17:5.) Abram became Abraham. The added syllable inserts the divine character in his name. Abraham means "father of a multitude." With God in our character, we can father and build a nation.

14. *Abraham sought a blessing for his children.* Men should seek a blessing for each of their children. Although Isaac was the child of promise, Abraham also sought a blessing for his rejected child, Ishmael, and received it. (See Genesis 17:18-20.) Parental blessings prevail.

Abraham Was Rewarded

God rewarded Abraham's faith, hard work and dedication to the covenant. In the book of Hebrews, key phrases appear, such as: "...Isaac and Jacob, the heirs with him of the same promise ...Therefore sprang there even of one...so many as the stars of the sky in multitude, and as the sand of the seashore innumerable" (Hebrews 11:9,12).

The clue to this father's greatness and the reason for God's favor upon him is found in Genesis 18:19:

> For I know him, *that he will command his children and his household after him,* and they shall keep the way of the Lord, to do justice and judgment; that the Lord may bring upon Abraham that which he hath spoken of him.

God blessed Abraham because he was a man who could be trusted to take responsibility for his dependents and faithfully plant God's Word in their hearts.

Many young men in the Bible disobeyed their fathers' teachings concerning God's Word. As a result, God swiftly cut off these potential "seeds of promise" and wiped out entire lineages! This happened to Eli and his disobedient sons. (See I Samuel 2:22-25.)

We ensure longevity and promise for our nations when we ensure the obedience of our children. Remember that God blessed Abraham because He could trust him, and He knew Abraham would command his sons to obey God's law.

Isaiah later reaffirmed those promises to Abraham's seed: "But thou, Israel, art my servant, Jacob whom I have chosen, *the seed of Abraham my friend*" (Isaiah 41:8).

God is still looking for "friends" like Abraham today, parents who will be partners with Him. Abraham's succeeding generations continue to be blessed by God to this day because of his friendship with God.

The future of your nation is bound to your obedience as a parent! Will you embrace the promises for your righteous seed?

10

Protect the Covenant

Instead of thy fathers shall be thy children, whom thou mayest make princes in all the earth.

I will make thy name to be remembered in all generations....

Psalm 45:16,17a

The battle for the seed continued to the cross and beyond, and the ancient enmity between God and Satan deepened. So has the bitter warfare between the bearers of righteous seed (godly parents) and Satan.

The enemy tries every strategy his evil mind can design, and he wants to deal a death blow whenever he can. Therefore, he always attacks the source of the seed — the parents. If he can corrupt the parent, then he will have successfully polluted or obliterated the ensuing seed.

Satan's real desire is to crush and pollute human offspring. One of his most effective tactics is to intrude into the sexual life of adults. He skillfully draws them and their society into adultery, sexual immorality, abortion, and perversion of every sort. Satan delights to see these sins destroy parents, because then their seed is polluted, crushed, hurt, or completely destroyed as well.

Satan works overtime to destroy every situation in which God is working to produce righteousness on the earth, and the Genesis 3:15 curse over him through the seed of woman is at the heart of it all. The seduction and destruction of parents is one of the devil's most effective methods to cut off the life source of the seed.

God knows every device in the enemy's arsenal, and He protects us from them — when we let Him. In Judges 13:4,13,14, God gave specific lifestyle and moral instructions to Manoah, along with His promise of a son. He was concerned about the purity of the parents because He knew it would affect the purity of the offspring.

God gave specific instructions to this couple so that their home and lifestyle would be holy before Him. Because of God's careful instructions and the obedience of Samson's parents, Samson seemed to have no conflicts or problems with double standards as he grew up. His parents faithfully obeyed the Lord's instructions and taught him to do the same in the Nazarite tradition.

God had specific standards for His chosen deliverer then, and He makes demands on the parents of righteous seed today! He calls us to holy living to preserve the seed and ensure that they attain their full spiritual inheritance and anointing for leadership.

What your seed is to become, you must be. Hard and rigid demands are often made upon us so we won't break or profane our covenant with God.

For the sake of the righteous seed, we should jealously guard the covenants and relationships God has ordained to maintain the purity of the seed.

Guard Against Seduction

Many of us say, "It could never happen to me. I'm a good parent and my marriage is strong." The Word of God can help us keep it that way! The Book of Proverbs describes the path of a young man on his way to death. He is void of understanding and wandering toward the street corner of the evil one. The seducer is waiting to flatter and entice him:

> **With her much fair speech she caused him to yield, with the flattering of her lips she forced him.**

Till a dart strike through his liver; as a bird hasteth to the snare, and knoweth not that it is for his life.

For she hath cast down many wounded; yea, many strong men have been slain by her.

Her house is the way to hell, going down to the chambers of death.

Proverbs 7:21,23,26,27

Notice the varied and extravagant preparations made by the prostitute. She not only attracts her victim with food and seductive sexual pleasure, she also adds some religion for good measure! She claims that she needs to fulfill her religious vows: "I have peace offerings with me..." (Verse 14)!

The enemy of the seed uses every trick or device imaginable to constrain, seduce and trap parents, the bearers of the seed. When he is successful, the result is usually dishonor, disease, or death, with inevitable consequences on the offspring, Satan's real target!

Avoid Unequal Yokes

Guard against any affiliation or covenant with people whose faith, lifestyle, and practices are contrary to those established by God for His children.

God told Abraham that His children were not to intermarry with foreigners. He said this to preserve the purity of heritage for the seed. Lovers and spouses who practiced a foreign religion often ensnared the Israelites and led them into false religious practices — including prostitution. (See Nehemiah 13:25,26.) This sexual tool was (and still is) one of the powerful snares the devil uses to trap carnal men and women.

This devilish tool had nearly swept through Israel in Numbers 25:1-3. These passages describe the whoredom Israel committed with idolatrous women of Moab and Midian. Prostitution was mingled with occultish worship and carnality of every sort. "...and the anger of the Lord was kindled against Israel" (Verse 3).

Everything came to a head when the rebellious Zimri committed a public act of sexual immorality at the very door of the tabernacle in the sight of Moses! This outraged Phinehas, the grandson of Aaron, the priest, who swiftly followed the couple into their tent, javelin in hand, and killed both of them — evidently in the very act of adultery! (See Verses 7 and 8.)

Phinehas, and his seed after him, were given a covenant of peace and an everlasting priesthood for his godly zeal.

Always remember that God is interested in protecting righteous seed. Don't fall into the trap described in Proverbs 2:17, which describes a whorish wife who "...forgetteth the covenant of her God." She renounced her marriage vows and was ensnared by false sinful practices.

Avoid Marital Unfaithfulness

The principal reason God instituted family relationships — including the marriage covenant — was to maintain the life and purity of the seed.

The importance of children in God's plan cannot be overestimated. Malachi 2:2-4 describes God's reply to the apostasy of His people and the irresponsibility of the priests. Notice the curse of judgment pronounced by God, "Behold, *I will corrupt your seed...*" (Malachi 2:3). God threatened annihilation to men who broke covenant!

God fulfilled His promises to Levi (Exodus 32:26-29) and Phinehas (Numbers 25:10-13). He fulfilled it through their righteous seed who continued to serve God as holy priests before Him.

Guard Against Pollution of Priestly Seed

Many people are reluctant to admit that God, at times, chooses to put an abrupt end to a man's lineage rather than allow his seed to disobey Him. This happened to the disobedient sons of Eli, the priest.

After Eli failed to bring his rebellious sons under control, God said, "But now the Lord saith...I will cut off thine arm, and the arm of thy father's house...and all the increase of thine house shall die in the flower of their age...thy two sons...in one day shall die, both of them...And I will raise me up a faithful priest ... and I will build him a sure house (generation)...." (See I Samuel 2:27-35).

God's judgment was swift and decisive. Eli's sons, Hophni and Phinehas, were both slain by Philistines on the same day. Eli died that day as well when he learned of the death of his sons and the capture of the ark of the Lord by the Philistines. God desires righteous seed and godly parents.

Malachi, the prophet, highlights the reason for God's radical judgment against marital unfaithfulness, saying: "And did he not make one?...And wherefore one? *That he might seek a godly seed.* Therefore take heed to your spirit, and let none deal treacherously against the wife of his youth" (Malachi 2:15).

God is seeking "godly seed." We must expect Him to purify and judge leaders and parents in His search for righteous seed. He is determined to preserve righteousness in our nations through our children.

Guard Jealously The Love Nest!

The cry of the Lord is that the marriage partner must be satisfied and rejoice with his spouse. His offspring must be produced and nurtured out of that joyful and pure relationship.

God calls us to a life of purity in marriage in Proverbs 5: "Drink waters out of thine own cistern, and running waters out of thine own well. . . Let thy fountain be blessed, and rejoice with the wife of thy youth" (Verses 15,18).

The Song of Solomon is God's marriage manual for man and woman. It is a continuous love song of two lovers in the marriage union. The atmosphere created by the lovers is one of anticipation, desire and yearning, mutually serving each other. It describes in detail the active and lavish preparations the lovers made for times of love together. There is always haste and movement, anointing of each other and hopeful expectation.

Lovers should always express rich commitment and mutual adoration to each other. God has ordained a togetherness and covenant between married lovers, lifelong friends. This is the atmosphere we must nourish as lovers and parents as we build the nest for the next generation. The best part of it all is that God, the instigator of it all, is well pleased!

11

Cry For Your Nation

The Lord shall go forth as a mighty man, he shall stir up jealousy like a man of war: he shall cry, yea, roar; he shall prevail against his enemies.

I have long time holden my peace; I have been still, and refrained myself: now will I cry like a travailing woman; I will destroy and devour at once.

Isaiah 42:13,14

As a mother, an educator, a Caribbean woman and leader in my nation, I have often found my heart breaking for various nations of the world. I weep for the hopelessness of the children and, yes, the helplessness of many parents and national leaders. But it is not a cry of despair!

Cry Like David Did

The Psalmist David once cried out to God in prayer, "...O God, forsake me not; until I have shewed thy strength unto this generation, and thy power to every one that is to come" (Psalm 71:18).

According to King David, there are two primary prayers or goals we are to strive for in life:

1. To show the Lord's strength to our generation.

2. To show His power and ability to the generation to come.

Selfish men or women think only of that which concerns their own well-being. Great men and women, like King David of ancient Israel, have an acute sense of history. They remember and understand the major events and people of the past, with vivid memories of the defeats and successes they represent (familial, cultural and national). They also have a keen sense of, and eye for, the future.

Great men and women are trans-generational. They span the generations:

1. **They reflect on the past and learn from it.**
2. **They act on the present and change it.**
3. **They plan for the future and actively work to build it.**

As Christians and as parents, we will have no lasting impact unless we do these things.

The urgent message of this book is simple and riveting: **the only thing that will last on this earth, after all is said and done, is what we have invested in our children.** Sometimes I like to think that the world actually belongs to them and that we are merely "on-lookers"! The mark of eternity, which is the seed of greatness, resides in men and women who are trans-generational in their thinking.

Live With An Eternal Perspective

Many of us have a mistaken or limited definition of eternal life. When we say, "When I was saved, I became a Christian and received 'eternal' life," we are referring to eternal life only as something stretching ahead of us without any end. But there is much more to eternal life than something we will experience some sweet day far away.

Eternal life is not locked into the future. *Eternal life is a quality of life.* It is a God-given perspective about life. God put it inside of us. God is eternal, and when we receive Jesus Christ as our personal Lord and Savior, *we inherit the potential to view life with an eternal perspective.*

It is God's will for us to enjoy a quality of life that has eternity in it. Jesus referred to this eternal quality of life when He said He came that we might have life, and that

more abundantly! (John 10:10.) Too many of us live short, ineffective lives, marked by spiritual short-sightedness and selfishness. This creates a problem not only for us and our generation, but also for our children and nation.

I believe an accurate paraphrase of the Psalmist David's cry would be, "Oh that I might change this generation, and oh that I might affect the next!"

God has shown me that the secret for becoming effective and great is to actively participate in changing the next generation.

When we become parents, we need to have a revelation of our partnership with God in raising up righteous seed. God wants to give us a deeper sense and quality of eternity in our hearts.

Jesus: The Ultimate Trans-Generational Man

Jesus said, "...I am the root and the offspring of David..." (Revelation 22:16). This statement reveals a complete sense of the past, the present, and the future.

Our Lord also said, "I am the Alpha and Omega, the beginning and the end, the first and the last" (Revelation 22:13). Jesus Christ continually displayed a supreme sense of generation, of history and of His pivotal place in time.

He has ordained that we do the same. I have a past, I have a present, and I may affect the future by the way I train my children and speak into the lives of the next generation.

God is looking for men and women with an eternal quality and perspective. Christ had that quality of eternity. The closer we get to God, the more we become eternal in our perspective and purpose.

Have An Eternal Perspective Like Jacob Did

A remarkable act with a supernatural perspective is described in Genesis 49:1, where Jacob gathered his sons together to bless them.

This chapter reveals that Jacob's blessings over his sons had an eternal and prophetic purpose.

> **And Jacob called unto his sons, and said, Gather yourselves together, that I may tell you** *that which shall befall you in the last days.*

In his blessing to each son, the patriarch foretold future events that would occur — always identifying them with each son's name, character and behavior. These blessings actually provide discerning Bible students with a preview of the history of the nation of Israel!

The truth becomes clear! Jacob actually foretold the *future of a nation* as it was *bound up in the future of his sons!*

You can determine the future history of your nation by the lives of your children. If you had five sons and you were to call them around you and say, "You, son, will be a law-giver; and you, as unstable as water, are going to serve your brother," your prophetic words upon them would, in effect, anticipate the history of your nation. How can this be? Your sons and daughters, like those of Jacob, make up your nation.

As the title of this book implies, we face a battle to see our children come to maturity and fulfill God's call upon their lives and affect their nation.

Jacob's older sons tried to snuff out the life of Joseph, their younger brother. But Jacob said to Joseph, "The blessing I give to you now will prevail above the curses of your brothers!" (Genesis 49:22-26, paraphrased.)

The results of Jacob's prophetic declarations over his sons should clearly illustrate the importance of our blessings on our children in this generation! In our mouth is the law of life. We can speak blessings that will prevail above the devices of the enemy.

This book presents strategies for Christian parenting, citizenship, the training of our children for nation building, and for the salvation of the nations through our seed.

The only way to understand the importance of our seed is to see that **God saves nations through the "righteous seed" (the anointed, separated and carefully trained children) of His people.** It has always been so, and it always will be!

God Himself Mourns For Nations. Mourn For YOUR Nation.

Most of us think of a nation as some big external phenomenon called a government or a society. It seems so impersonal that we wonder how anyone could talk so emotionally about a nation. We would never cry for it. Yet God Himself mourns for sinful nations and asks godly women to wail and cry for their nations.

In Jeremiah 9:20,21 the prophet pleads:

> ...**teach your daughters wailing, and every one her neighbour lamentation.**

> **For death is come up into our windows, and is entered into our palaces,** *to cut off the children from without, and the young men from the streets.*

People who become vital and influential in their nation can determine its history. Since our sons and daughters — and the godly way of life we have taught them to live — are on the line in this battle with the devil over nations and people, we had better take an active interest in the life of our nations. We make up our nations. **The enemy is after our seed because he knows that the future of our nations is dependent on them.** If he can succeed in spoiling them, then our nations don't stand a chance.

God has put eternity within us. We have an eternal word for our nations. Our children's heritage and our blessings upon them shape the future.

I travel extensively through the Caribbean, the United States and Europe. As I visit the various cities in these nations and regions, I often pray, "God, show me the heart of this nation." I can't escape the sense of the spiritual decadence and depravity that prevails. You may think that your nation is not as ungodly as another, but it may be perilously close.

God's judgment may come suddenly, violently and intrusively, such as His destruction of Sodom and Gomorrah, or of Jerusalem as Jesus prophesied. Most often, it is a natural consequence of disobeying His eternal laws.

When a nation, a people or society rejects or strays from God's principles of right behavior and government, then a slow but sure deterioration of standards follows, along with a steady disintegration of its culture. Nearly always, the most noticeable symptom of decay is the insidious vulgarization of the life of the people.

Talk to people who knew your nation years ago and ask them to compare those conditions with what they see now. Will they not tell you that there is an enormous and marked difference? Will they say, "Oh for the good old days!"?

Whether you examine your nation's history through God's perspective, or indeed through the eyes of a casual observer, you will begin to understand how much your nation has changed — in most cases, for the worse!

Rebellious and blatant sin, on an individual or institutionalized (public) scale, whether subcultural or national, always produces inevitable results in the life and history of a nation and the families who comprise it.

The blessings we speak and the standards we set for our children today will determine the direction of our nation and the direction of the generations of tomorrow. Isaiah 61:9 says, ''And their seed shall be known among the Gentiles, and their offspring among the people: all that shall see them shall acknowledge them, that they are the seed which the Lord hath blessed.''

God has invested a precious and immutable promise in the seed of godly parents. He literally promises that your offspring will be known throughout America, Europe, or India or any other nation or continent they are called to affect. All that see them shall acknowledge that they are *the seed that the Lord hath blessed.*

As Christian parents, our prayer should be: ''Father, let our children be known, not for the sake of being popular, but known for the word that they speak, of repentance to the nations; and may they be known for the kingdom life they live and establish in their nations.''

12
Midnight In The Nations

Thus saith the Lord, As the new wine is found in the cluster, and one saith, Destroy it not; for a blessing is in it: so will I do for my servants' sakes, that I may not destroy them all.

And I will bring forth a seed out of Jacob, and out of Judah an inheritor of my mountains: and mine elect shall inherit it, and my servants shall dwell there.

Isaiah 65:8,9

It is midnight in the nations. If you do not believe me, walk the streets of your nation tonight. Look at all the children and young adults entangled in works of darkness. The enemy is working overtime to kill our seed! While the cities sleep, youth roam their streets impelled by the magnetic force of Satan's seed traps.

My life changed when God gave me a picture of my nation. I saw women in trouble crying for their sons, refusing to believe that their children could really be involved in drugs. I saw children killing each other in fits of jealousy, fighting and rivalry. I saw children neglected, abused and hungry.

The book of Exodus describes God's dealings with hardhearted Pharaoh, whose sole intention was to enslave and oppress the children of Israel.

At midnight God struck His most potent blow in His battle for the seed:

And Moses said, Thus saith the Lord, About midnight will I go out into the midst of Egypt:

> And all the firstborn in the land of Egypt shall die, from the firstborn of Pharaoh that sitteth upon his throne, even unto the firstborn of the maidservant that is behind the mill; and all the firstborn of the beasts.
>
> And there shall be a great cry throughout the land of Egypt, such as there was none like it, nor shall be like it any more.
>
> **Exodus 11:4-6**

God had warned Pharaoh about this tragedy earlier through Moses. He made it clear that if he didn't release His people, then his own firstborn son would die, along with the firstborn in every household in Egypt (not covered by the blood). (See Exodus 4:22,23.) This incident wasn't simply a battle of wills, it was a battle for the seed! The heart of the Father God is greatly stirred in defense of His children, our children.

Exodus 12:2-13 signaled the beginning of a new season for captive Israel. God moved at the midnight hour. First, He warned the congregation of Israel to sacrifice a lamb for each household and place the blood on the doorposts of each house.

> And the blood shall be to you for a token upon the houses where ye are: and when I see the blood, I will pass over you, and the plague shall not be upon you to destroy you, when I smite the land of Egypt.
>
> **Exodus 12:13**

That night, the avenging angel killed the firstborn of every household, including Pharaoh's. God is determined to preserve righteous seed, and national sin reaps consequences for the youth of any nation.

Exodus 12:30 gives us a vivid and pathetic picture of the great mourning that rose in Egypt that night, "...and there was a great cry in Egypt...."

Women have mourned over their children at other times as well. Jeremiah 31:15b and Matthew 2:18 speak of

Rachel who "would not be comforted," mourning for her children.

Even later, mothers cried for their children after the ruthless Herod ordered "the Slaughter of the Innocents" in a vain effort to snuff out the life of the newborn King Jesus, the Seed of Promise (See Matthew 2:13-20).

A nation that has sown corruption will reap corruption. We have abused and neglected our children and let them drink deeply of the cup of corruption. God is about to pour out His wrath, and He is saying, "Everyone who is not under the blood will suffer. You will lose your children if you refuse to follow My instruction for their preservation."

We may see a time of separation, when only the enemy's seed will be destroyed; but the time may come when our own seed may also suffer hurt and death. As Abraham's nephew, Lot, discovered in the city of Sodom, the results of community or national sin often affect ALL members of that society. Our children may suffer the consequences of God's judgment on our nation — unless we act now!

Let us take a stand for righteousness and God's righteous seed! Satan has no right to take or oppress any seed, whether that seed belongs to us, to Pharaoh, or to Egypt! We have a responsibility to pray for their salvation and deliverance from the hand of the enemy. We are saying, "Any child born in this nation is to be God's child, and at midnight when God's wrath is extended, we want *all* those children safe under the blood of the Lord Jesus Christ."

God says that we must do something. We must take a lamb and sprinkle the blood: "And ye shall observe this thing for an ordinance to thee and to thy sons for ever" (Exodus 12:24).

Did this intercessory responsibility — the anointing with the blood of the lamb over the godly seed — end with the Israelites in ancient Egypt? No! It is midnight in our nations now. God says we must observe the passover on behalf of our sons forever, under the new covenant of the Lamb. It is a call for national intercession.

Mothers and fathers, grandparents and godly teachers, we have a responsibility to present the blood of Jesus Christ to each child. I believe God is saying to us today, "Every mother needs to know how to lead a soul to Christ, because her major responsibility is to lead her own sons and daughters to Christ." Mother, do you know how to point your young child to Jesus?

The man (husband) has the primary responsibility to lead his household to Christ and to sprinkle the blood. To put the blood on the lintel means *to lead your own children and household to Christ*. This is the call of God to all parents.

God told the Jews in Exodus 13:2, "Sanctify unto me all the firstborn, whatsoever openeth the womb among the children of Israel, both of man and of beast: it is mine."

God is calling us to sanctify, to set apart our children as holy and sacred. I believe He has a special word for our firstborn, because if we learn to dedicate our first child (the one we so often idolize!) to God, we will be careful to sanctify all of our children.

God is calling us to sanctify and set apart our children unto Him. He is saying, "Separate these children of Mine. They will bring My Kingdom to this nation."

Exodus 13:3 says, ". . . Remember this day, in which ye came out from Egypt, out of the house of bondage; for by strength of hand the Lord brought you from this place: there shall no leavened bread be eaten."

I'm sharing this verse because God is saying to us, "In your homes, there must be holiness unto Me, symbolized by *no leavened bread*. Remember: there are some things that must not happen in your home, because you have set apart and separated your children for My Kingdom."

When Samson was born, God said, "Do not put a razor to his head: give him no wine or strong drink." There were specific rules for raising Samson. We also saw that there were specific rules for Samson's mother: "Do not drink any wine or strong drink." (See Judges 13:4,14). There are to be specific rules regulating behavior in our homes.

As women, we have nations in our wombs, and we are bringing up sons and daughters who will inherit the promises of God — children who have the call of God upon them. God wants mothers to ensure their own integrity and the integrity of their homes through a chosen lifestyle of holiness.

Micah 2:9 says, "The women of my people have ye cast out from their pleasant houses; from their children have ye taken away my glory for ever." That is what the enemy does. He steals God's glory from our children. We must reclaim that glory.

Our cry should be the cry of Jeremiah, "Behold the voice of the cry of the daughter of my people...For the hurt of the daughter of my people am I hurt...Is there no balm in Gilead; is there no physician there? Why then is not the health of the daughter of my people recovered?" (Jeremiah 8:19-22).

When the children of a nation are being destroyed by Satan, the mothers experience the greatest pain and hurt. But there is a balm in Gilead. It is found in the God who feels even more deeply the pain created by the death and destruction of His sons and daughters, our children. And He waits to answer our cry for their deliverance.

I pray that God will pour out upon us the supernatural ability and strength of character we need as godly men and women to be nation builders! I pray that He will make us strong and tall in our nations; that He will open our eyes to see the seed of righteous nations we have within our homes right now.

The blessings we give to our children are blessings for the nations. I pray that we will seek God until the Spirit be poured out from on high. I pray for the fulfillment of the promises given through Zechariah, "And I will pour upon the house of David (God's children today), and upon the inhabitants of Jerusalem, the spirit of grace and of supplications..." (Zechariah 12:10).

As Jesus bore the cross towards Calvary, He said, "... Daughters of Jerusalem, weep not for me, but weep for yourselves, and for your children" (Luke 23:28). I pray that God will give us that kind of heart; that our eyes will see the weakness, the sinfulness, and the vulnerability of our seed and that we will weep before the Lord in intercession for our children.

One great promise for our seed in particular should be confessed daily over our children. It is found in Isaiah 54:13, "And *all* thy children shall be taught of the Lord; and great shall be the peace of thy children."

Remember: the life of a great man or woman is wrapped up in the life of the nation. God is interested in godly men and women who conceive and nurture sons and daughters who will redeem their nation.

God's character is trans-generational. We are to imitate our Heavenly Father. We should possess that quality and live with a perpetual sense of history and destiny. Our future is wrapped up in our children's ability to inherit God's promises. Your seed is Righteous Seed, and your children must rise up to take the Gospel of the kingdom to your nation and the nations of the world.

May the God who Himself has a great love for our children continue to equip us with supernatural strategy to save our children. May He bestow upon us the determination to daily conquer the enemy and to lay hold on victory in the BATTLE FOR THE SEED.